Love

ETERNAL THEMES IN ART
FROM BOTTICELLI TO KAHLO

Love

Brad Finger

PRESTEL
MUNICH · LONDON · NEW YORK

CONTENTS
Eternal Themes in Art

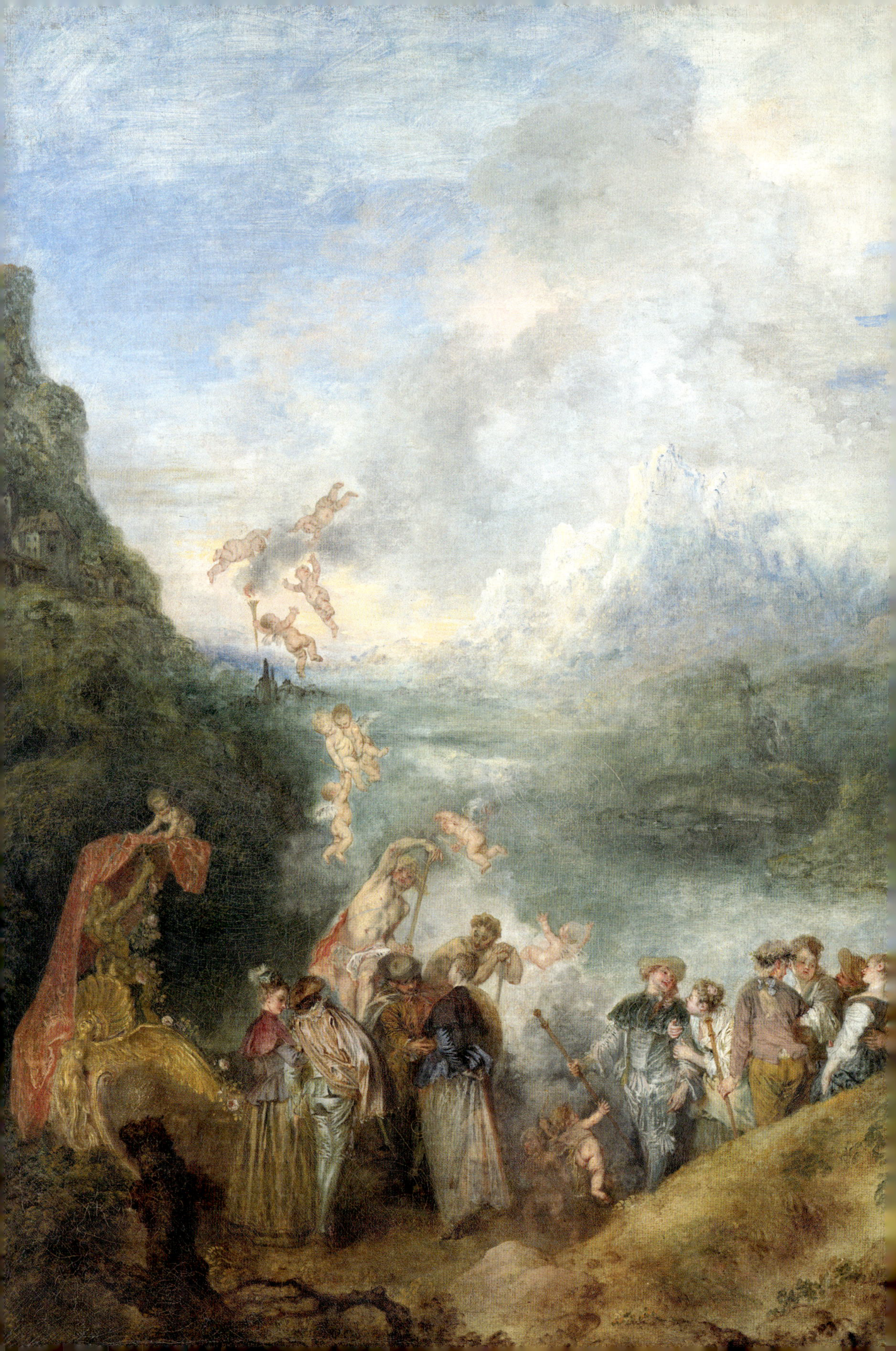

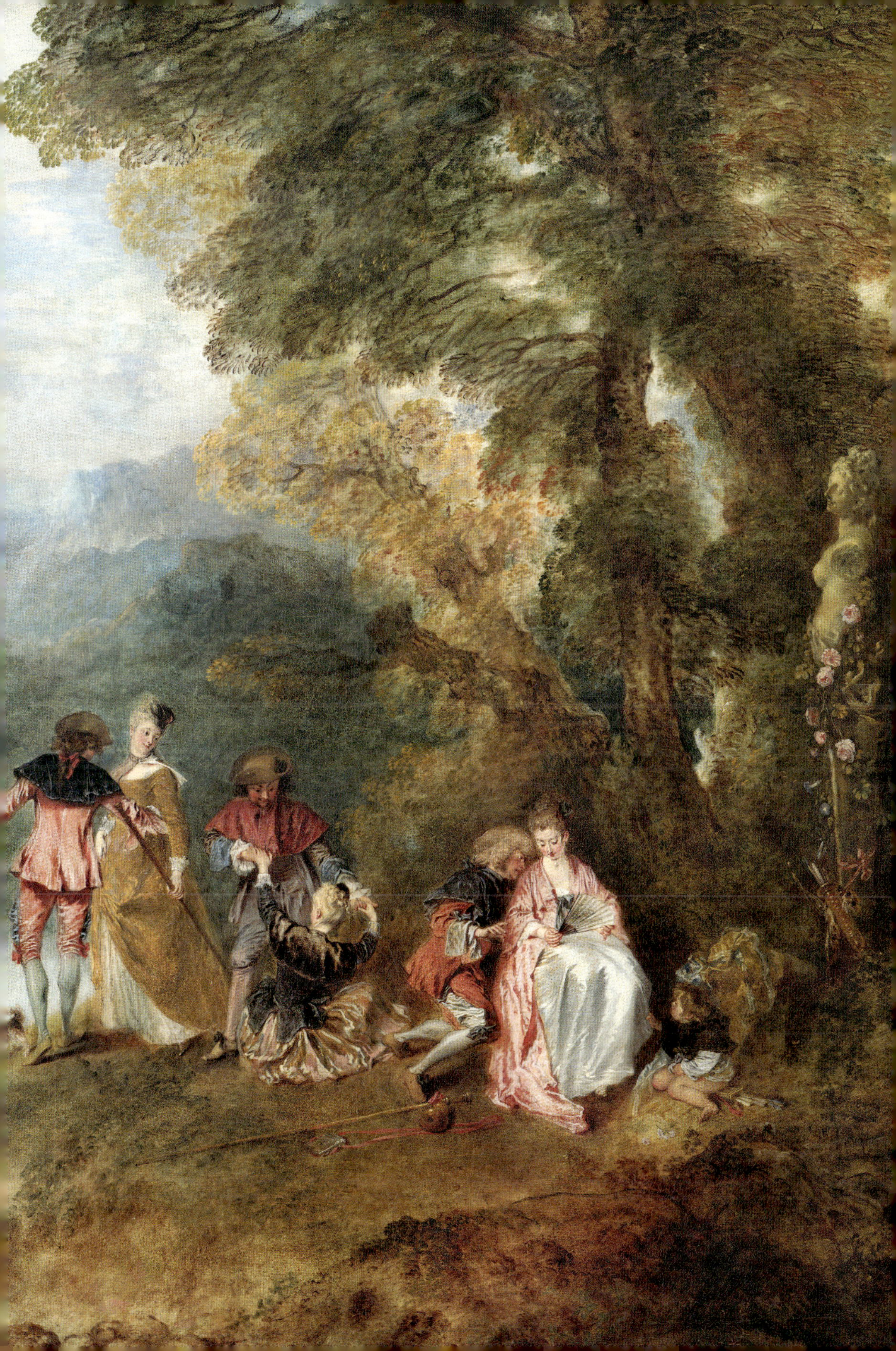

INTRODUCTION

Art and love: two words that have been linked together for centuries. But has the idea of love always meant what it means to us today? German poet Johann Wolfgang von Goethe (1749–1832), with his revolutionary novel *The Sorrows of Young Werther* (1774), may have helped define our modern notion of love. Written as a series of letters, the story tells of a young legal clerk named Werther who falls in love with Charlotte, a country woman engaged to another man. Smitten with her at first sight, Werther becomes unable to cope with his place in Charlotte's life – one whose feelings can never be truly returned. In the end, he decides to commit suicide rather than live with the pain of love unfulfilled.

Tales of star-crossed lovers had been written long before *Werther*, most prominently in William Shakespeare's tragic play *Romeo and Juliet* (premiered 1597). But Goethe explored as never before the psychological impact of love: the feelings of possessiveness, the extreme highs and lows and the loss of emotional control. Such feelings were drawn from Goethe's own 'storm and stress' experience of unrequited love (with his own 'Charlotte', Charlotte Buff); and they would inspire many nineteenth-century writers of the 'Romantic' age.

Goethe's era also marked a turning point in how love was depicted in art. Earlier generations of artists had visualized love in symbolic form – such as the classical Roman goddess Venus, personification of erotic love, or the biblical figures of Adam and Eve, symbols of God's love for humankind in Judaism and Christianity. Non-Western artists, too, often represented love as externalized beings, such as in the Hindu images of Radha and Krishna, deities who represent the ideal nature of devotion between man and woman. But after 1800, artists in many parts of the world began depicting love as something much more personal and internalized, something more intimately human.

The evolution of love in art began thousands of years ago. Wealthy couples in ancient Egypt had monumental sculpted 'portraits' made for their tombs. Both husband and wife were rendered in stiff, formal poses, either seated or standing, in order to show the eternal nature of their union. This tradition was briefly subverted by the Pharaoh Akhenaten (died c. 1334 BC), who had his artists portray him and his wife in more informal poses, even playing with their children. Akhenaten's images were among the first to depict familial love in realistic terms.

Later ancient civilizations in Greece, Rome and India began to explore the erotic side of love. Greek and Roman sculptors, for example, represented the human body with unparalleled accuracy, enabling them to emphasize the sensual qualities of their gods and goddesses – deities whose stories featured explicit, and often violent, sexual escapades. This type of body worship extended to everyday decorative art in private homes. Domestic wall frescoes discovered in Pompeii, in southern Italy, for example, show Amor and other gods in openly erotic positions.

Never did I dance more lightly. I felt myself more than mortal, holding this loveliest of creatures in my arms, flying with her as rapidly as the wind, till I lost sight of every other object; and O Wilhelm, I vowed at that moment, that a maiden whom I loved, or for whom I felt the slightest attachment, never, never should waltz with any one else but with me, if I went to perdition for it! [...] We took a few turns in the room to recover our breath. Charlotte sat down, and felt refreshed by partaking of some oranges which I had had secured [...] but at every slice which, from politeness, she offered to her neighbours, I felt as though a dagger went through my heart.

JOHANN WOLFGANG VON GOETHE,
THE SORROWS OF YOUNG WERTHER (1774)

With the fall of Rome in the fifth century and the rise of Christianity in Europe, sexual 'openness' in art was replaced by more elevated, moralistic illustrations of love. Illuminated manuscripts began picturing stories of medieval courtly romances. Originally sung by travelling poets called troubadours or minnesingers, these love poems described gallant knights and their worship of idealized women with unblemished moral characters. At the same time, medieval painters captured scenes from the Bible that spoke to God's undying love for humanity, often through the sacrifices of biblical figures such as Job or Jesus Christ. For medieval artists, love had become a spiritual conception, one that involved a spiritual journey.

The strong cultural hold of the Church began to weaken in the fifteenth century, when the Renaissance flowered in northern Italy and spread to large parts of Europe. It began a renewal of interest in nature and the human body, as well as the art and literature of ancient Greece and Rome. Classical gods of love, such as Aphrodite and Eros, Venus and Cupid, began to reappear in the work of Italian painters like Sandro Botticelli (c. 1445–1510) and Titian (c. 1488/90–1576). Artists also began to highlight the lives and loves of ordinary people. Netherlandish painters like Jan van Eyck (c. 1380/90–1441) and Pieter Bruegel the Elder (c. 1525/30–1569) captured rural weddings and matrimonial portraits in minute, realistic detail. At around the same time, the wedding ceremony itself began to take its modern shape. In 1563, Catholic leaders at the Council of Trent formally ratified marriage as a sacrament, one requiring two witnesses and a priest.All of these innovations led artists to think of new ways of expressing love on the canvas. Flemish artist Peter Paul Rubens (1577–1640), for example, captured his own marriage with remarkable candour. He and his wife Isabella Brant (1591–1626) carry an affectionate, casual air about them, despite their formal attire. Traditionally, marriage had been viewed as an economic or political necessity – the union of two suitable families. But here we see two people who seem to enjoy a true friendship, a real love match. Other artists of the seventeenth and eighteenth centuries focused on love as a more fleeting, or even frivolous, pursuit. Jean-Honoré Fragonard's *The Swing* (c. 1767/68) is a veritable tribute to flirtation. The woman on the swing plays the role of a coquette, gracefully kicking off her shoe in the air, revealing a little more than her foot to arouse her lover below. But the painting's stylized figures and theatrical gestures present love (especially erotic love) as artificial and misleading.

Works of the Rococo period, like *The Swing*, enjoyed relatively brief popularity. Soon, they were ridiculed as products of a dissolute, out-of-touch upper class. Social and political elites were losing legitimacy among Europe's intellectuals, as an array of cultural and scientific advances took place. The Industrial Revolution began to spawn a larger, urban middle class with money and time to spend; while Enlightenment thinkers like Voltaire (1694–1778) and Jean-Jacques Rousseau (1712–1778) offered stinging criticism of traditional religion and monarchical government – criticisms that led to political revolutions in the Americas and France. Amidst all of this change, artists and writers began to explore intense, personal feelings in their work, including love and desire. The Romantic era in art was born, as was the age of Romantic love.

Goethe's *Werther* became an integral part of the new age. Its intense, and sometimes destructive, passions inspired artists of all stripes. Goethe's countryman, for example, the painter Caspar David Friedrich (1774–1840) captured strong emotions in nature and in the way people in his art interacted with the natural world. His *On the Sailing Boat* (1818–1820) presents a young couple on a journey – both literal and spiritual – at sea. As in *Werther*, the work draws inspiration from the artist's own experiences of love (in this case, Friedrich's marriage to Caroline Bommer). The painter employs dramatic perspective and evocative colouring to suggest both the uncertainty and the adventure of a young romance.

Personal reflections of love would become a staple for artists in the succeeding generations. During the nineteenth century, for example, romantic passion often became wrapped up with patriotic fervour. In Milanese painter Francesco Hayez's *The Kiss* (1859), for example, a passionate couple represents both love and a call for independence for the newly emerging nation of Italy. Not long afterwards, artists in France, led by Édouard Manet (1832–1883), would proclaim their own 'independence' from the stuffy Paris Salon. So-called 'Exhibitions of Rejects' began in 1863, helping to create a new category of 'outsider' artist. Among these were Impressionist painters like Manet and Pierre-Auguste Renoir (1841–1919), who often captured love as an evocative, fleeting moment on the dance floor or in a sun-dappled café.

Elsewhere in Europe and America, even more radical styles of art developed as the twentieth century dawned. Expressionist artists, including Norwegian painter Edvard Munch (1863–1944) and Russian painter Marianne von Werefkin (1860–1938), portrayed love as an often-painful evolution – a giddy, love-struck first embrace transforming into disillusionment and malaise. It was an art influenced by writers like Sigmund Freud (1856–1939) and August Strindberg (1849–1912), whose works reflected new ideas about human psychology and the deep-seated roots of human desire. Other movements captured love in more surreal or non-realistic ways. The American Surrealist Man Ray (1890–1976) used a disembodied pair of lips to express his overwhelming sense of loss after a break-up. Swiss-German modernist Paul Klee's *Eros* (1923) reduced the very concept of love – and the joining of man and woman – into a series of abstract triangular forms and subtle progressions of colour.

Through these pioneering works of early modernism, artists gained the freedom to portray love in almost any way they wished. Keith Haring (1958–1990) used simplified, comic-book figures to celebrate the formerly marginalized romantic love of the LGBTQ community; Serbian artist Marina Abramović (born 1946) and her former partner Ulay (1943–2020) performed gruelling 'endurance' art to probe how love is shared between two people; while Pop artist Robert Indiana (1928–2018) showed us how the very word 'love' (and the shapes of its letters) could stir up surprising emotional responses.

On the following pages, we will discuss fifty images that illustrate the progress of love in art over three thousand years. Like the emotion itself, images of love are ever-changing, yet they also capture something deeply rooted in time.

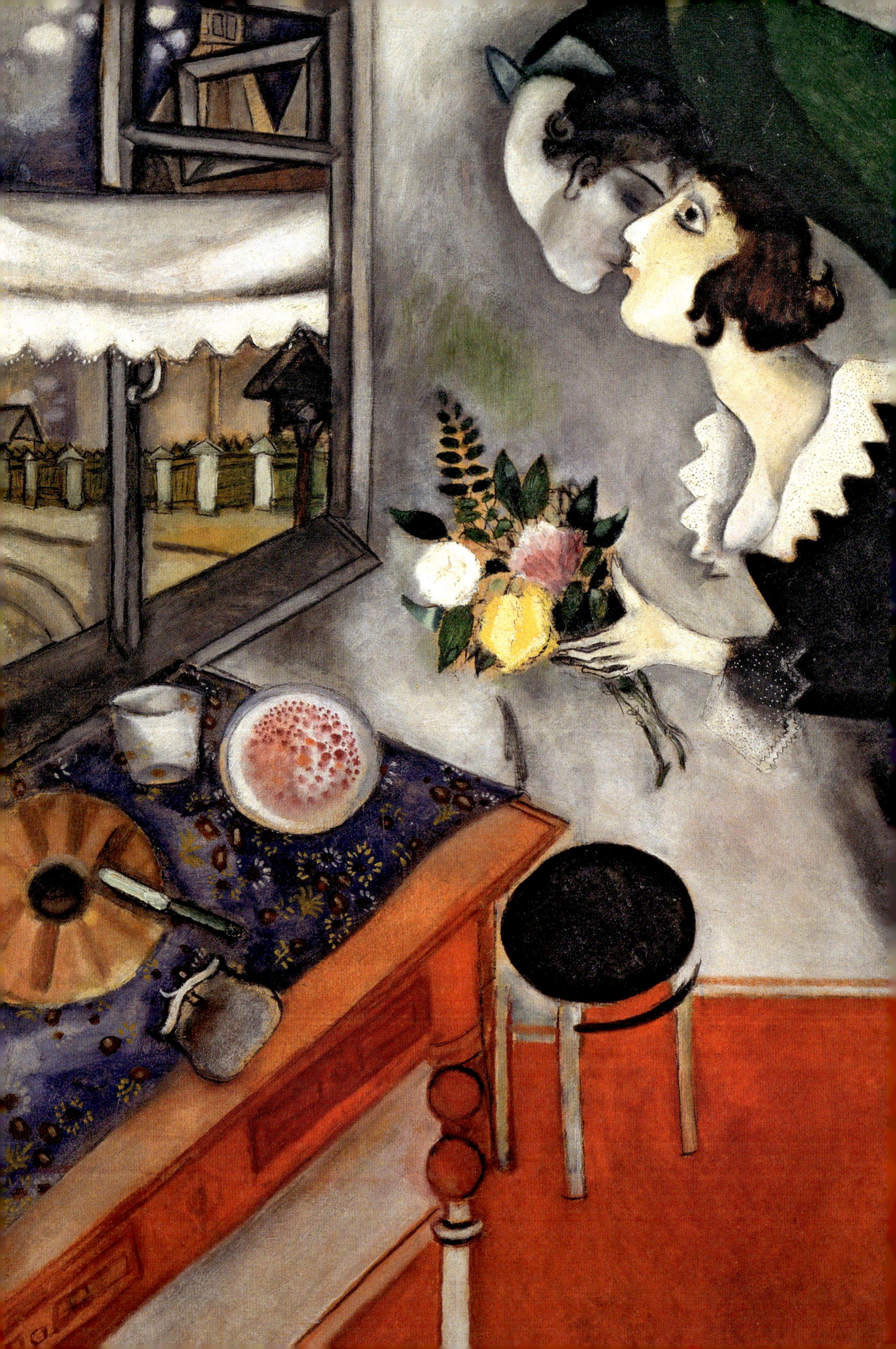

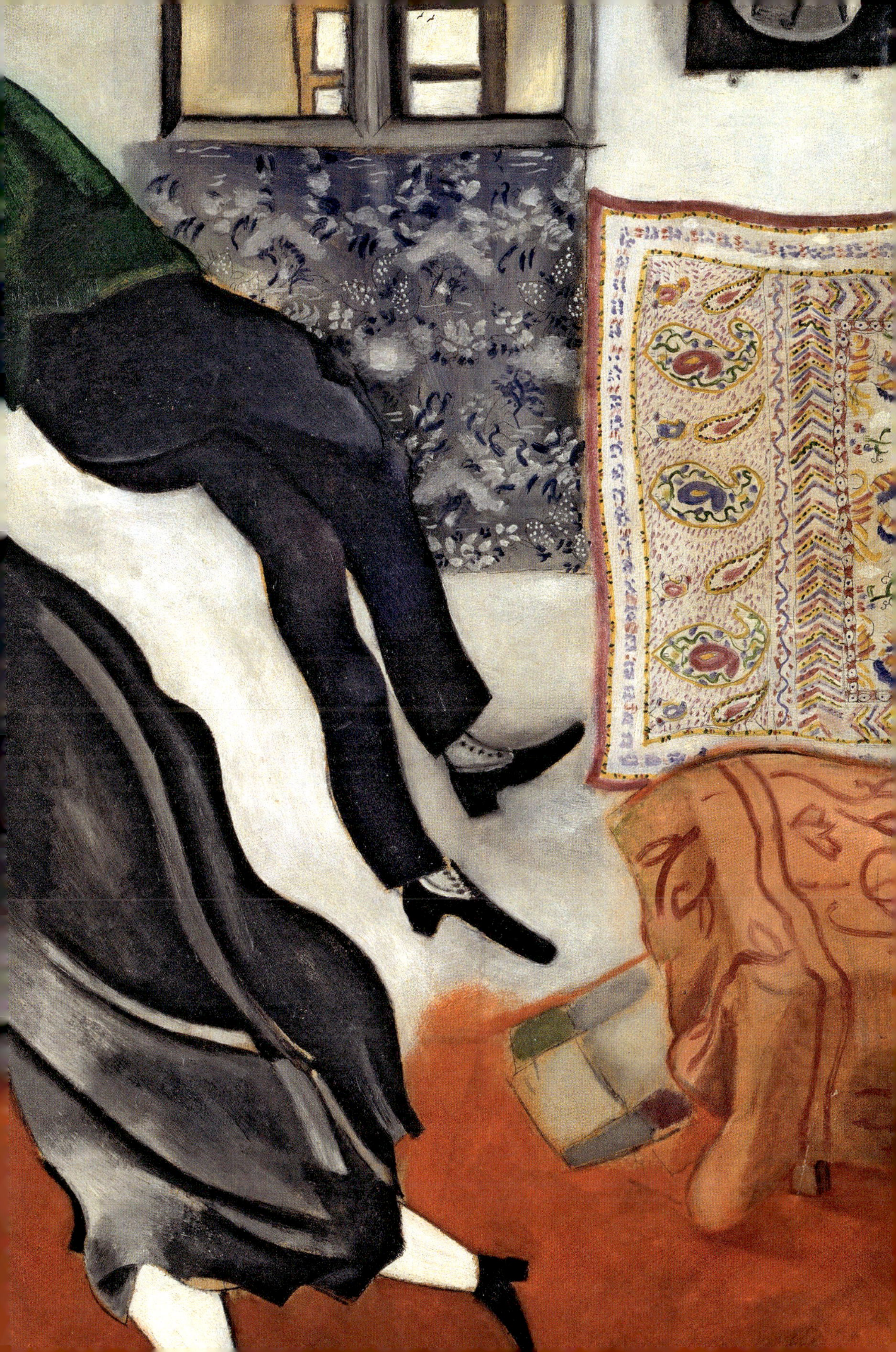

ANONYMOUS AMARNA CARVER

mid-14th century BC

This god goes where he pleases and no one else knows his going. I approach him, the things which he has made. How exalted they are.

AKHENATEN (c. 1350 BC),
RECORDED ON A PYLON AT KARNAK

Artworks that touch upon love, marriage and family go back thousands of years. One of the first civilizations to make monumental artworks, the ancient Egyptians, captured pharaohs and other prominent people in stone sculptures and stelae (upright carved slabs used for religious or commemorative purposes, occasionally as in this case as altars in homes). Sometimes featuring double portraits of husbands and wives, these images were traditionally stiff and formal in appearance. Egyptians wanted to present themselves as timeless and grand. Such practices, however, changed radically during the reign of one pharaoh in the mid-1300s BC, during what is known as the New Kingdom. He took power as Amenhotep IV, but during his reign he decided to transform much of what Egyptian culture had been. Abandoning the traditional Egyptian faith, which featured many gods, Amenhotep IV established a new religion based on a single sun god, Aten, whose image, like the sun, was a disc or sphere in the sky. The pharaoh then changed his name to Akhenaten, which can be translated as 'Aten is pleased', and built a new capital city called Amarna. There his artists would develop a radical, new style of art.

Few surviving works depict the new 'Amarna' style better than this stela, which features Akhenaten, his wife Nefertiti and three of their daughters (Meritaten, Meketaten and Ankhesenpaaten). Gone are the rigid, idealized poses of earlier centuries. We now see the ruler and his queen in a more affectionate, informal way, holding and kissing their children. The artist also shows off a new manner of rendering his subjects' bodies. Limbs have become thinner and more stylized, bellies are more rounded and heads – especially those of the children – appear oddly elongated. Everything, in short, seems more vibrant and expressive, possibly as a way of celebrating the creative powers of their new sun-disc god Aten, which we see sending down its rays upon the royal family. Works like this represent one of the first recorded artistic revolutions – one often centred around family love and devotion. But the revolution would be short-lived. After Akhenaten's death, his young heir Tutankhaten would restore the old religion and eliminate the word 'Aten' from his name, making it Tutankhamun.

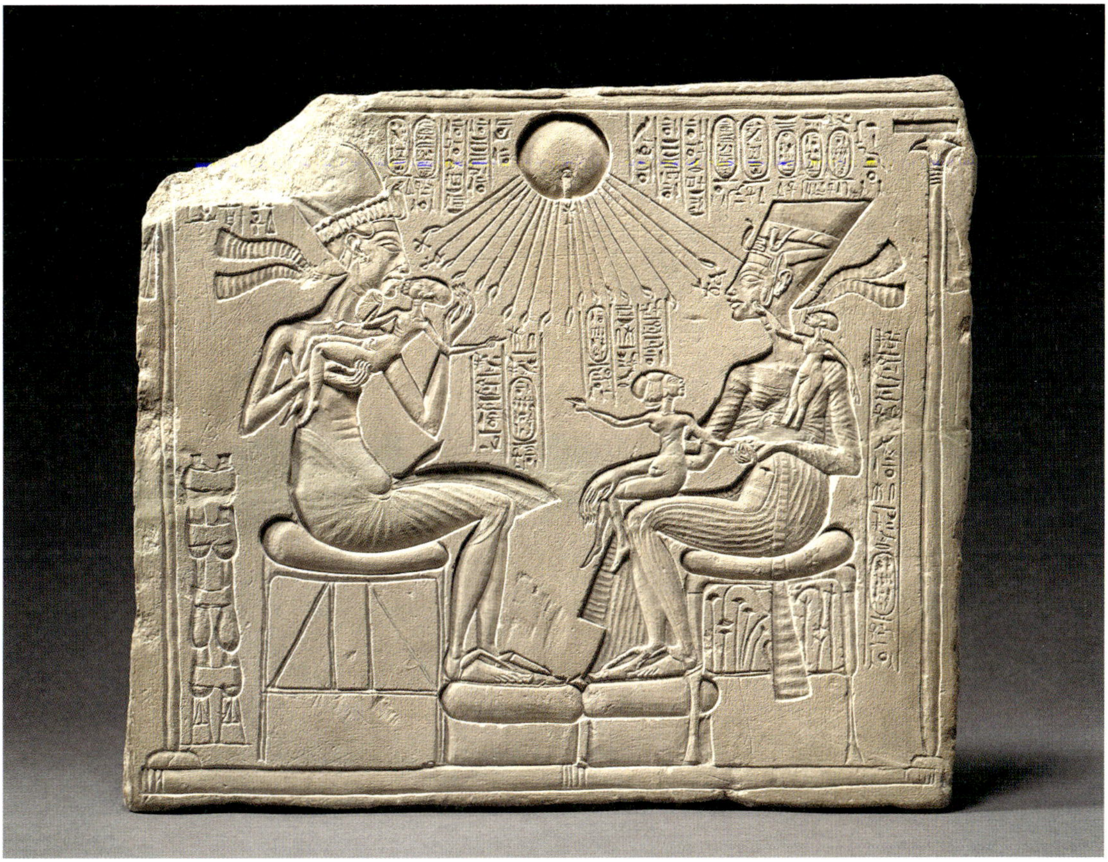

Akhenaten and His Family, c. 1351–1334 BC, limestone,
33.5 × 39.5 × 3.5 cm (13 ¼ × 15 ½ × 1 ⅜ in.), Egyptian Museum and Papyrus Collection, Berlin

ANONYMOUS HELLENISTIC SCULPTOR
c. 150–100 BC

[We] entered the temple. In the midst thereof sits the goddess –
she's a most beautiful statue [...] arrogantly smiling a little as a grin parts her lips.
Draped by no garment, all her beauty is uncovered
and revealed, except in so far as she unobtrusively uses one hand
to hide her private parts. So great was the power of the craftsman's art
that the hard unyielding marble did justice to every limb.
Charicles at any rate raised a mad distracted cry [...]
And, as he spoke, he ran up and, stretching out his neck as far as he could,
started to kiss the goddess with importunate lips.

AN ANCIENT SATIRIST, *AFFAIRS OF THE HEART*,
TRADITIONALLY ATTRIBUTED TO LUCIAN (2ND CENTURY AD)

Love in ancient Greece and Rome was intimately bound up with art. More than any civilization before it, ancient Greeks worshipped the human body and did all they could to recreate it accurately in their sculptures and paintings. For Greek sculptors, a statue of a god or goddess could do more than inspire religious devotion. It could also arouse powerful emotions – including sensual desire and love.

Perhaps the most celebrated ancient Greek sculpture was made for a temple in the city of Knidos (modern day Tekir in southwestern Turkey). Created in the fourth century BC, this image of Aphrodite, goddess of love and beauty, stood in a small, open-air temple. The sanctuary had a roof and colonnade, but no walls, enabling people outside the building to view Aphrodite from all sides. What made the work so remarkable was its depiction of a life-size female nude. Until that time, only male gods, heroes and athletes were portrayed nude in monumental Greek art. What is more, the Aphrodite of Knidos was rendered to look both real and enticing. Its sculptor, Praxiteles, gave the goddess a soft, somewhat seductive posture, covering her groin with one hand while reaching for a drapery to cover herself with the other. Her position was also slightly twisting (a pose known as *contrapposto*), meant to be admired from all angles. Aphrodite was a marvel of artistry, one that, according to ancient sources, made marble look like polished, living flesh. A later text from the Roman Empire, titled *Amores* or *Affairs of the Heart*, relays a humorous tale of male travellers who were so overcome by this Aphrodite that they tried to kiss and even have sex with it.

Today, Praxiteles's original sculpture is lost. We only know about it through ancient texts and copies made by later artists. One of the best surviving copies is a bronze statuette now at the Metropolitan Museum of Art in New York. Made between 150 and 100 BC – during the Hellenistic period, 323–30 BC – the statuette gives us some idea, in miniature, of Praxiteles's irresistible image of divinely carnal love.

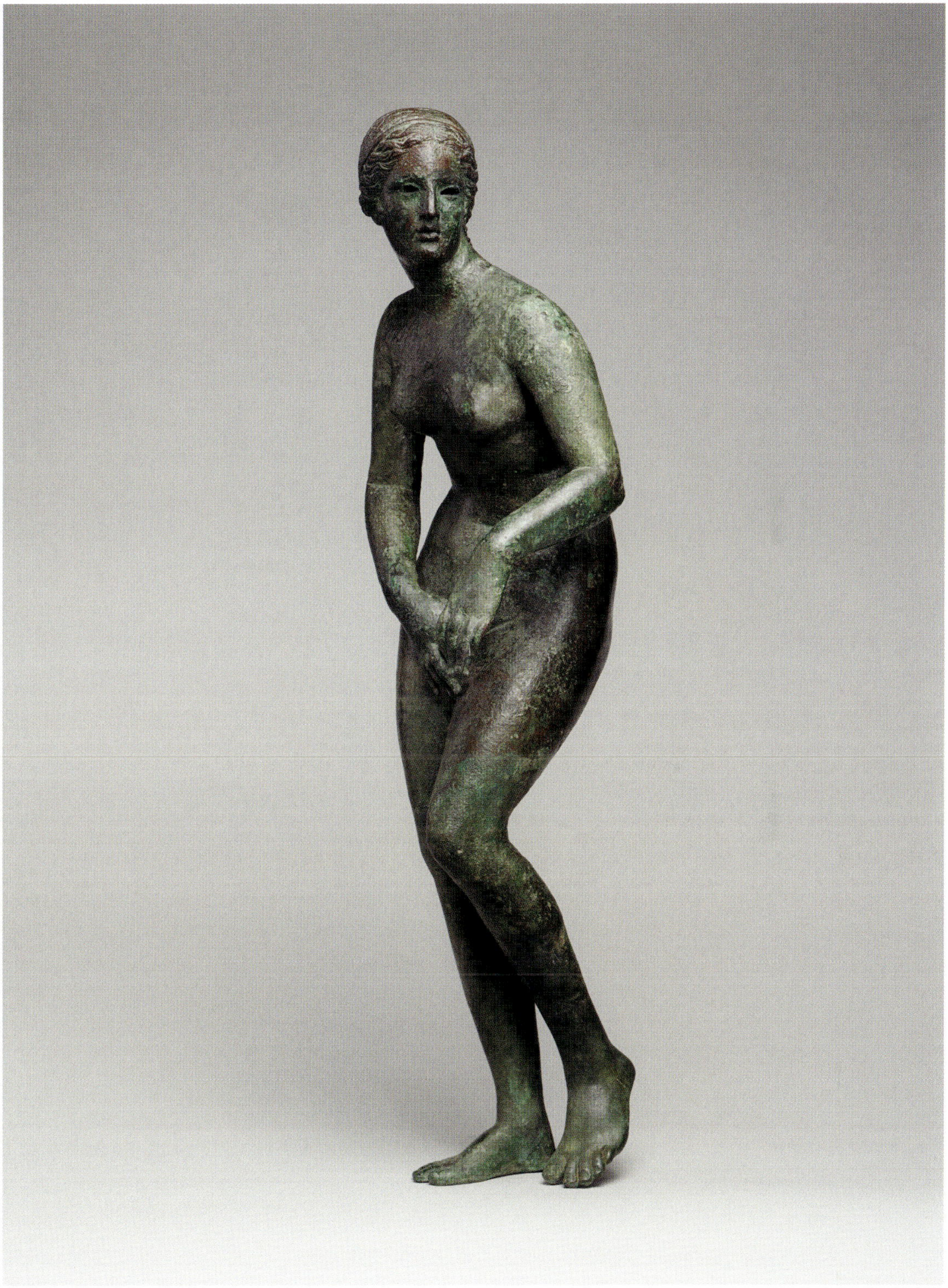

Bronze Statuette of Aphrodite, after the *Aphrodite of Knidos*, c. 150–100 BC, bronze, height 51.7 cm (20 ⅜ in.), The Metropolitan Museum of Art, New York

ANONYMOUS ROMAN FRESCO PAINTER

mid-1st century AD

With the help of her lover, Psyche completed the tasks set for her by Venus; and at last, [...] taken up into heaven, she enjoyed a perpetual marriage with Cupid, to whom she bore a daughter named Pleasure.

GIOVANNI BOCCACCIO,
GENEALOGY OF THE PAGAN GODS (1360)

Apuleius (c. AD 124–after 170), an ancient Numidian (North African) author, tells the dramatic love story of Amor and Psyche in his bawdy novel *The Golden Ass*. Psyche is a princess whose beauty has been praised as the equal of goddess Venus. She has even acquired followers who wrongfully worship her instead of Venus, which has incurred the jealousy of the vain deity. Venus decides to have her son, Amor (god of love), also known as Cupid, shoot Psyche with an arrow that will make her fall in love with an ugly creature. However, he fails in his mission and ends up accidently piercing himself so that he becomes smitten with Psyche. From this follows a complex tale, where Psyche is carried away from her home by Zephyr (a god of wind) to a beautiful palace. There she sleeps in a darkened room with someone she cannot quite see – someone who turns out to be Cupid himself. She then finds herself under the power of Venus and must carry out several trials for the goddess, including a voyage to the underworld. After the last trial, Psyche is sent into a deep sleep, only to be awakened by Amor and taken to Mount Olympus, where an assembly of the gods approves of her marriage to him. Psyche is given ambrosia, a drink granting her eternal life; and the story ends when she gives birth to a daughter, Voluptas, which is Latin for 'Pleasure'.

Apuleius's version of the tale was 'rediscovered' by Renaissance authors like Giovanni Boccaccio (1313–1375), and it has become the best-known version today. But the story is likely many centuries older. Archaeologists have found images of Amor and Psyche that predate Apuleius's time. One of them was discovered in Pompeii at the house of a wealthy tradesman named Terentius Neo. Dating from just before Pompeii was buried by the eruption of Mount Vesuvius in AD 79, this small fresco shows the mythological couple in an almost aggressively sensual embrace. As historians have discovered in places like Pompeii, Roman families often possessed art that depicted love and sexual passion in explicit ways. After the fall of Rome in the fifth century AD, such images would not be seen in European art for more than a millennium.

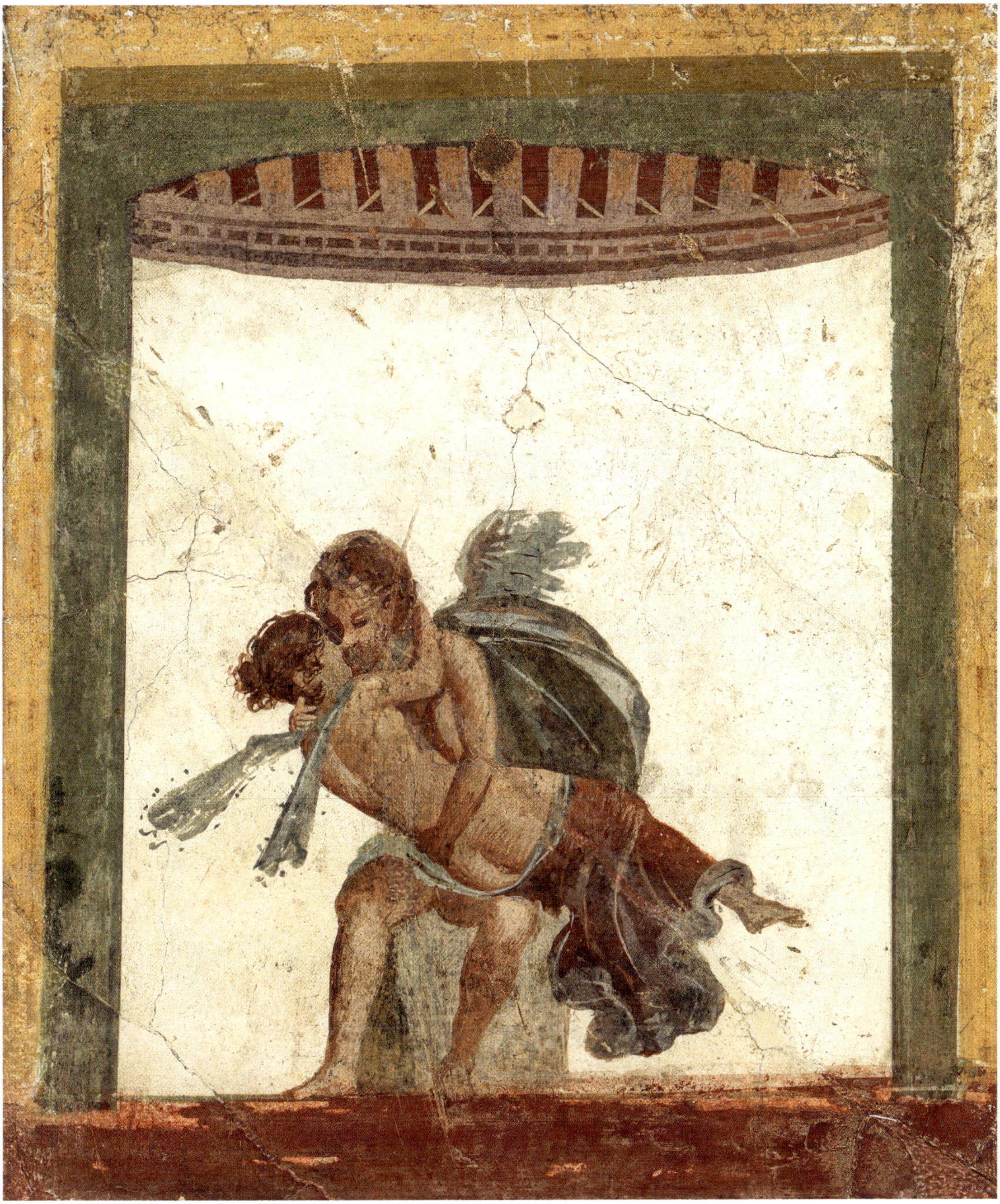

Amor and Psyche, c. AD 60, fresco from Pompeii,
55 × 47 cm (21 ⅝ × 18 ½ in.), Museo Archeologico Nazionale di Napoli, Naples

MASTER OF THE CODEX MANESSE

early 14th century

All other women fade from sight.
Never on earth have I looked on one with such delight.
Her eyes shine clear as a star.
In dew, what flower was so fair to behold as my lady,
whom I crown in song?

KONRAD VON ALTSTETTEN,
'I HAVE SENT MY HEART TO THE BELOVED' (c. 1325)

Artists from the European Middle Ages, a period dominated by the Christian Church, nearly always focused on stories from the Bible. But there were exceptions to this rule – exceptions that had to do with love! A new kind of performer emerged in Europe around 1100, one that travelled from town to town singing poems about idealized, courtly romance. These artists went by different names depending on the country from which they came. In France and along the Mediterranean, they were known as troubadours, while those from Germanic lands were called minnesingers. Some of the love songs (or *Minnesang*) they performed are known today because they were preserved in exquisite illuminated manuscripts. In the *Codex Manesse*, a stunning document from the fourteenth century, we find illustrated love poems meant to be sung by a number of different authors, including Konrad von Altstetten (active c. 1320–1327), a poet from what is now eastern Switzerland.

The *Codex Manesse* image shown here depicts Konrad von Altstetten in an embrace with his female lover. The large flowering rose bush, which seems to sprout from Konrad's lap, may represent the Tree of Jesse – a biblical image from the Old and New Testaments often linked to fertility and procreation in medieval art. Scholars also believe Konrad's falcon may represent the 'taming' of sexual passion. Such themes of love and sexual desire, made more vivid by the artist's rich colours, reflect the passion in Konrad von Altstetten's lyrical poetry. It is a visual expression of a love more beautiful than any flower 'in dew'.

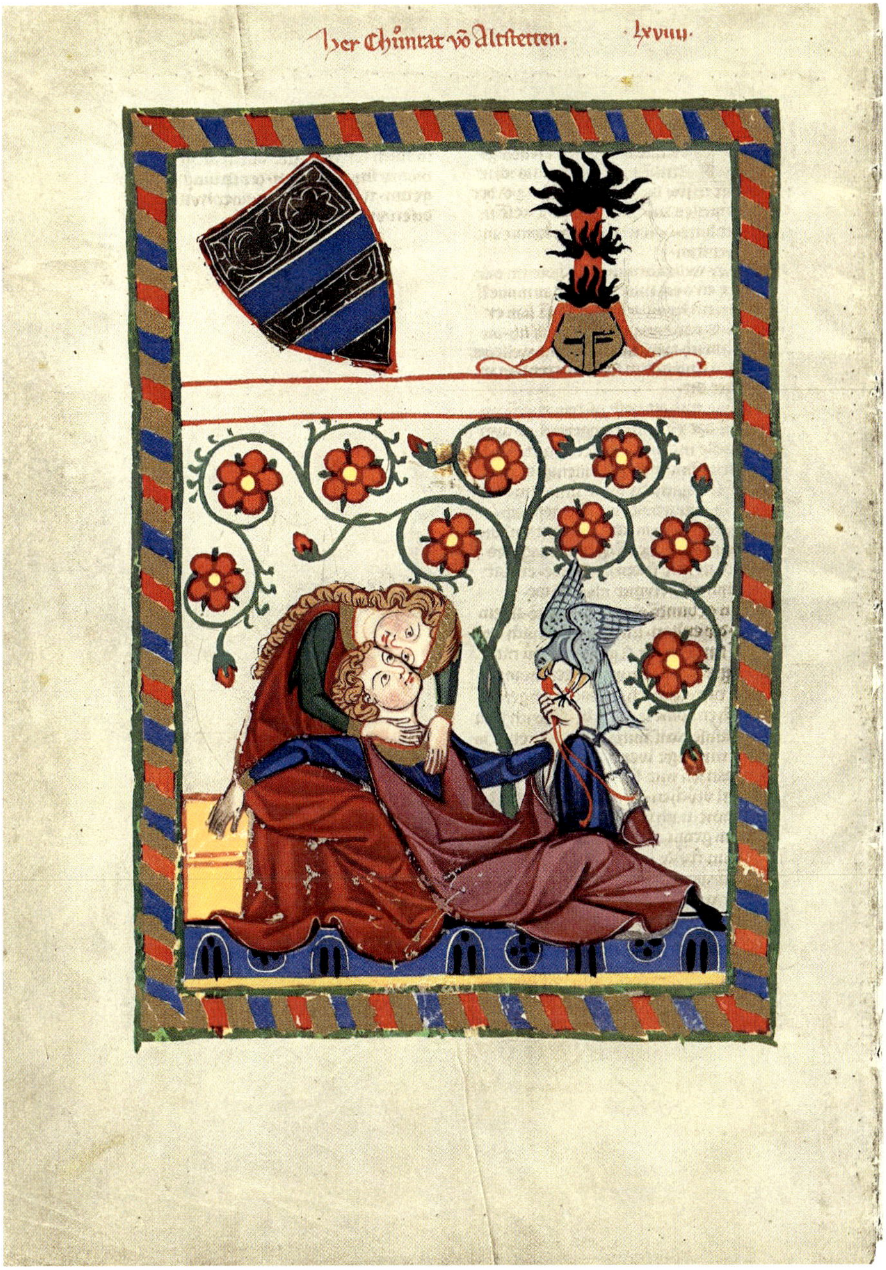

Herr Konrad von Altstetten, from the *Codex Manesse*, c. 1304 – c. 1340, illuminated parchment, 35.5 × 25 cm (14 × 9 ⅞ in.), Heidelberg University Library, Heidelberg

JAN VAN EYCK
c. 1380/90–1441

From her to you comes loving thought
that leads to highest good, while you pursue it [...]

PETRARCH, *IL CANZONIERE* (c. 1327–c. 1368), SONNET 13

Love and marriage are on display in this minutely detailed portrait by Flemish painter Jan van Eyck. But the exact identity of the people – and the true meaning of the artwork – remain a mystery. Van Eyck shows us the bedroom of an affluent man's house in Bruges, a city in Flanders (now Belgium), in 1434. For many years, beginning in the 1850s, art historians believed the picture to depict a wedding. They argued that the man with the hat and ermine-trimmed velvet cape was Giovanni Arnolfini, member of a wealthy Italian merchant family that had a branch of its business in Bruges. Arnolfini traded in expensive fabrics and other costly items, and records show Giovanni had been living in Bruges since childhood. Historians also believed the lady in the green gown, with the intricately worked sleeves, to be Arnolfini's bride, Giovanna Cenami. Recent scholarship, however, suggests that Arnolfini and Cenami were married as late as 1447, well after Jan van Eyck's death, and that the gentleman in the hat may instead be a relative of Arnolfini and his wife.

It is also now unclear whether this painting depicts a wedding ceremony at all. In the fifteenth century, marriage vows did not need to be exchanged in a church. Instead, couples would promise to be faithful to each other in front of witnesses at home. During the ceremony, the bridegroom would offer his bride his right hand. This picture, however, appears to show a 'left-handed' or 'morganatic' marriage. Such weddings only took place between a couple of unequal status. Yet the bride in this painting looks directly at her 'husband' and not towards the ground, as a woman of unequal birth would do in such a marriage. Moreover, we know that both Arnolfini and Cenami were from prosperous families. Such inconsistencies raise doubts as to the exact meaning of the work.

Nevertheless, the 'Arnolfini portrait' remains one of the most important images of love in Western art. Van Eyck was a leading artist of the Northern Renaissance, a part of the Renaissance centred in Flanders and other countries north of Italy. With his remarkable talent for accuracy and naturalism, Van Eyck brings this tender moment to life in ways artists had not been able to do in the Middle Ages, when paintings were more stylized and much less personal. Here we see two 'real' people in a moment of tenderness – a reality further emphasized by all of the fine details, from the softly rendered folds of the clothes and bedspreads to the reflection of the couple seen in the room's convex mirror. Van Eyck seemed to know the importance of this picture when he painted it. Above the mirror on the back wall you can read in bold Gothic script 'Johannes de eyck fuit hic 1434', which is Latin for 'Jan van Eyck was here 1434'.

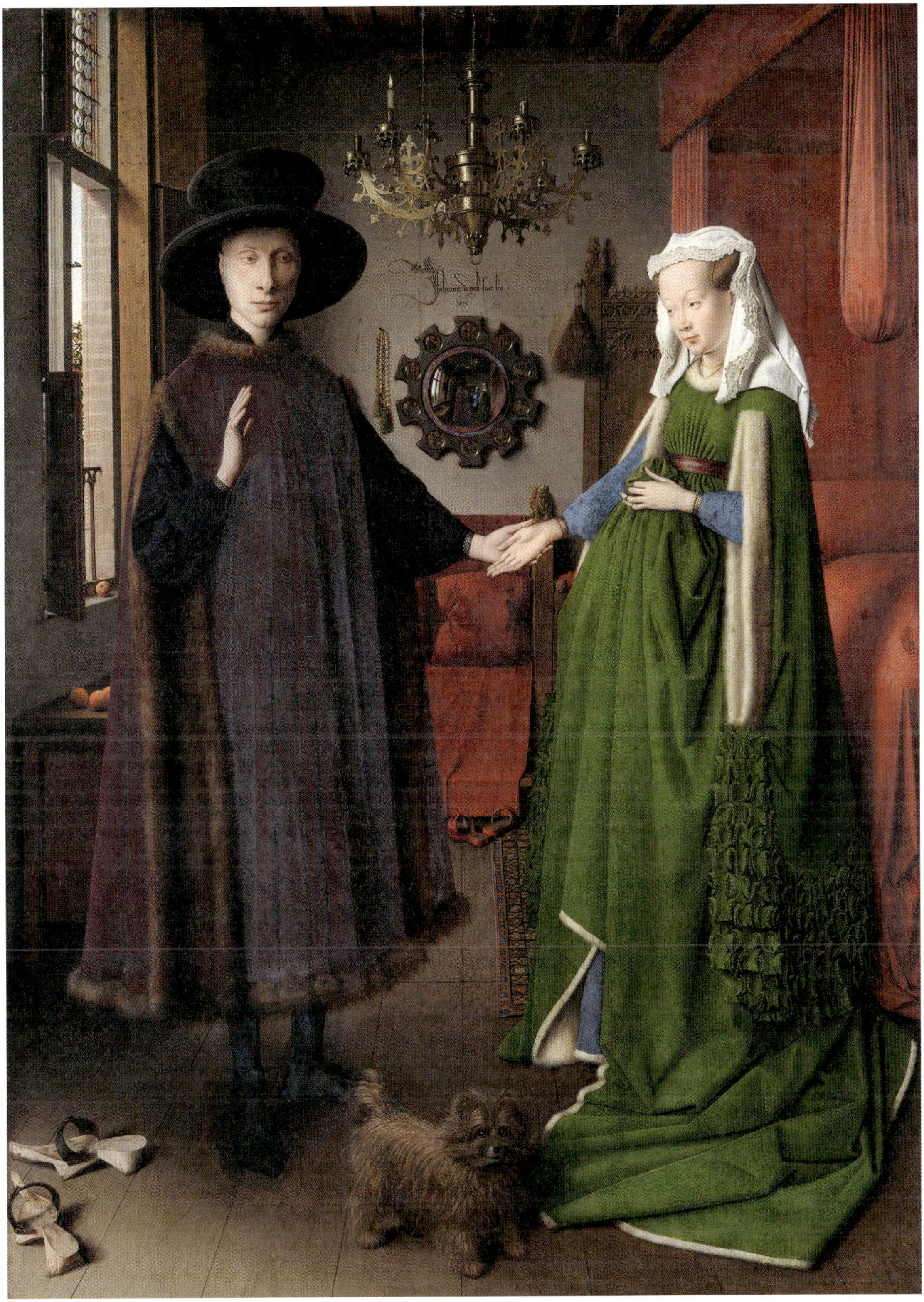

The Arnolfini Portrait, 1434, oil on panel (probably oak),
82.2 × 60 cm (32 ⅜ × 23 ⅝ in.), The National Gallery, London

SANDRO BOTTICELLI
c. 1445–1510

Muse, tell me the things done by golden Aphrodite,
the one from Cyprus, who arouses sweet desire for gods
and who subdues the races of mortal humans [...]

HOMERIC HYMN TO APHRODITE
(c. 7TH CENTURY–c. 6TH CENTURY BC)

With the birth of the Renaissance, artists began to depart from Christian messages of divine love, or the courtly love of the troubadours, and to rediscover more 'profane' stories and images from the ancient world. Few artworks better represent this change than Sandro Botticelli's *Birth of Venus*, one of the first large-scale paintings of Greco-Roman mythology since the fall of Rome.

Botticelli was born Alessandro di Mariano di Vanni Filipepi, son of a tradesman in Florence. His father, Mariano, began work as a gold-beater, producing gold leaf, shortly after Sandro was born, and the young Florentine was exposed to artists and craftsmen at an early age. After an apprenticeship with the painter Fra Filippo Lippi (1406–1469), Sandro soon established his own studio, where he acquired commissions from the most prominent families in Florence, including the ruling Medici family. Indeed, it was likely the Medici who commissioned this painting.

The Birth of Venus has been considered a masterpiece since the 1500s, when it was praised by artist and historian Giorgio Vasari (1511–1574). On a grand scale, it displays the painter's use of vibrant colour, graceful lines and expressive form – a mix of realism and fantasy. The nude central figure of Venus (the Roman name for the Greek goddess Aphrodite) seems to float above her giant scallop shell. She is being 'blown' to shore by Zephyr and Aura, two mythological wind deities seen hovering above her from the left. Waiting for Venus on shore is a Hora, a divine attendant of Venus, with an elaborately embroidered dress for her to wear. The Hora may also represent springtime, as her own dress is covered in a floral motif. All of these figures – rendered in a weightless, supernatural way – provide a stunning illustration of the Venus story. Wealthy Florentines at the time would likely have understood Venus as the goddess who inspired sensual love in humankind through her physical beauty.

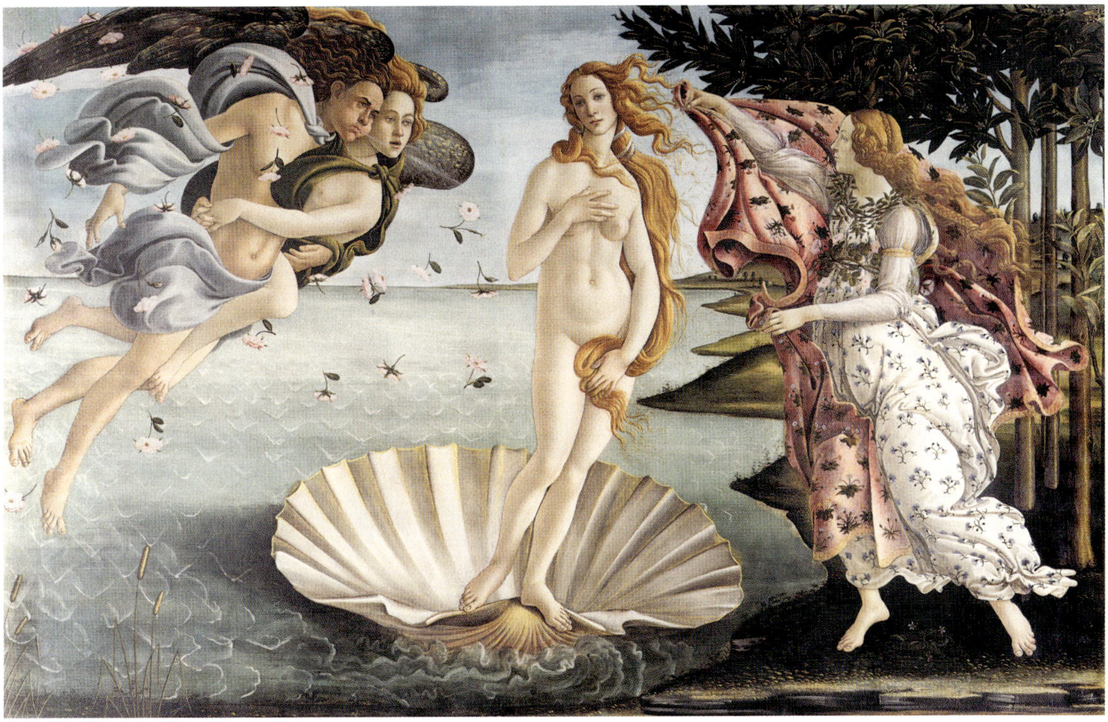

The Birth of Venus, c. 1485, tempera on canvas,
172.5 × 278.5 cm (67 ⅞ × 109 ⅝ in.), Gallerie degli Uffizi, Florence

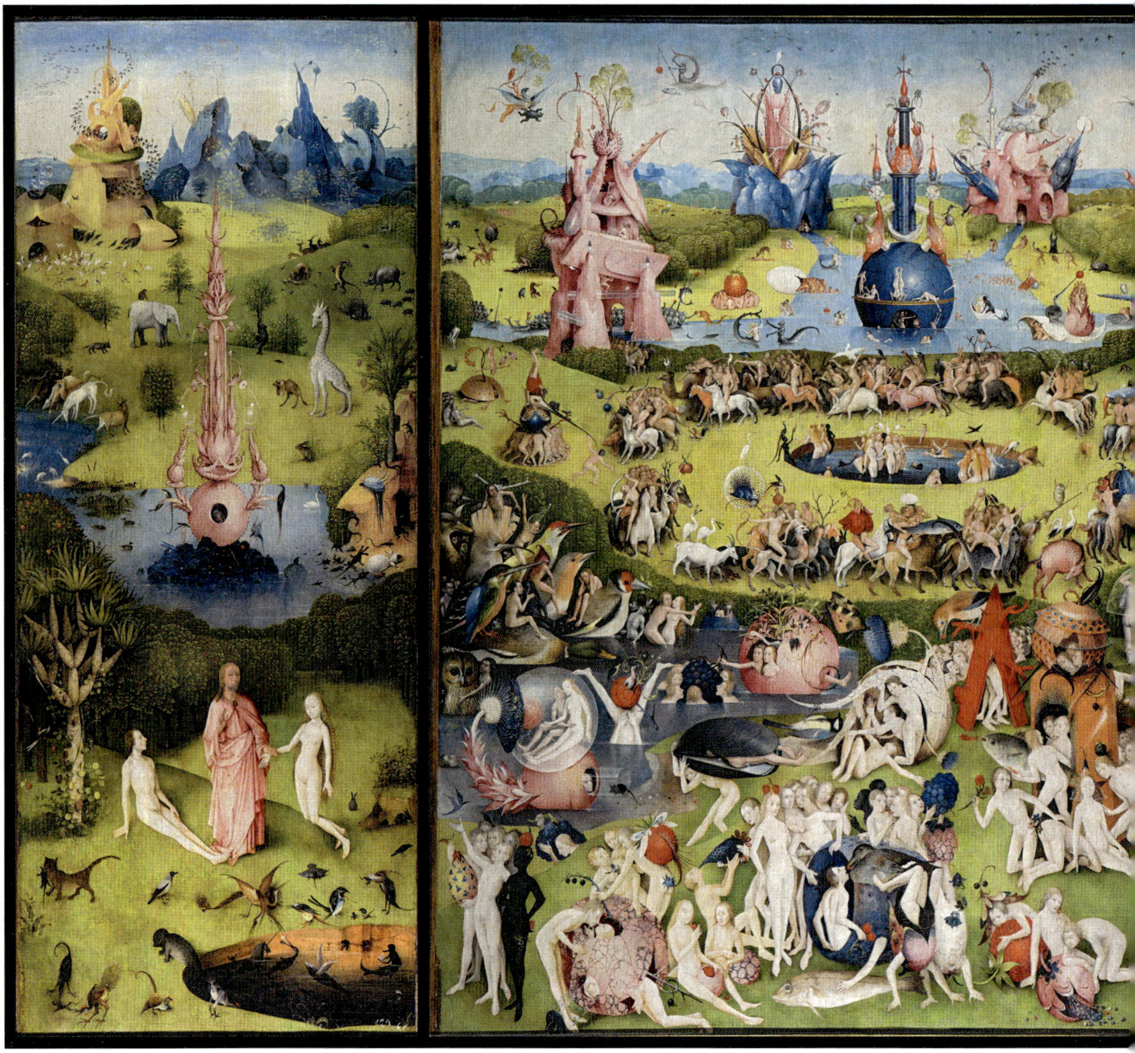

HIERONYMUS BOSCH
c. 1450–1516

The Lord saw how great the wickedness of the human race had become on the earth, and that every inclination of the thoughts of the human heart was only evil [...]

GENESIS 6:5

Love and lust have been subjects of Christian art for centuries. During the late Middle Ages and early Renaissance, religious artwork portrayed lust and sexual desire as sinful pursuits that could lead humankind away from the true love of God. Medieval attitudes about sexual desire are captured dramatically in *The Garden of Earthly Delights*, a monumental triptych (a three-panelled picture, often associated with altarpieces) by Netherlandish painter Hieronymus Bosch.

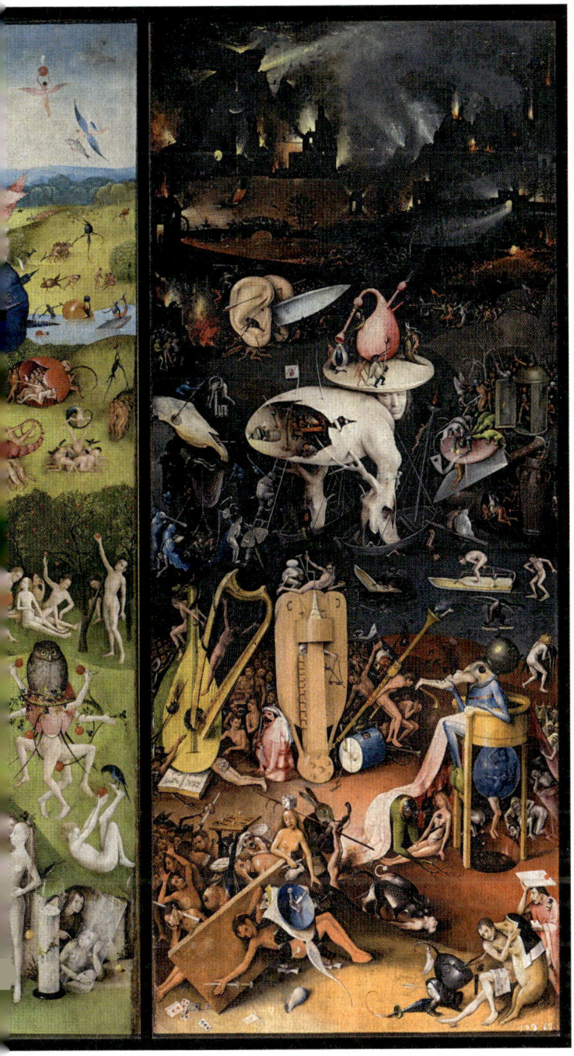

The central panel lies directly between wings showing images of innocence (the Garden of Eden) and damnation (Hell), and it depicts humanity in a kind of middle kingdom – one full of sinful revelry. Modern scholars have interpreted this image as a deceptive paradise, a false garden of temptations. Human figures, like those shown in the following detail, are rendered in the same naked state as Adam and Eve, but their nakedness is no longer a sign of innocence. The people have warped God's command to 'be fruitful and multiply', using it as an excuse for lechery and debauchery. Fifteenth-century folklore often incorporated birds and fruits as symbols for sexual deviance. In this panel, the descendants of Adam and Eve are portrayed unclothed and enjoying ripe strawberries, one of which is grotesquely oversized – a reference to oversized sexual appetite. The giant owl may represent spiritual darkness and the rejection of God. Bosch's work, a remarkable combination of fantasy and naturalism, is a world of indulgence that can only lead to a hellish fate.

The Garden of Earthly Delights, 1490–1500, oil on oak, 205.5 × 384.9 cm (80 ⅞ × 151 ½ in.), central panel 185.8 × 172.5 cm (73 ⅛ × 67 ⅞ in.), Museo Nacional del Prado, Madrid

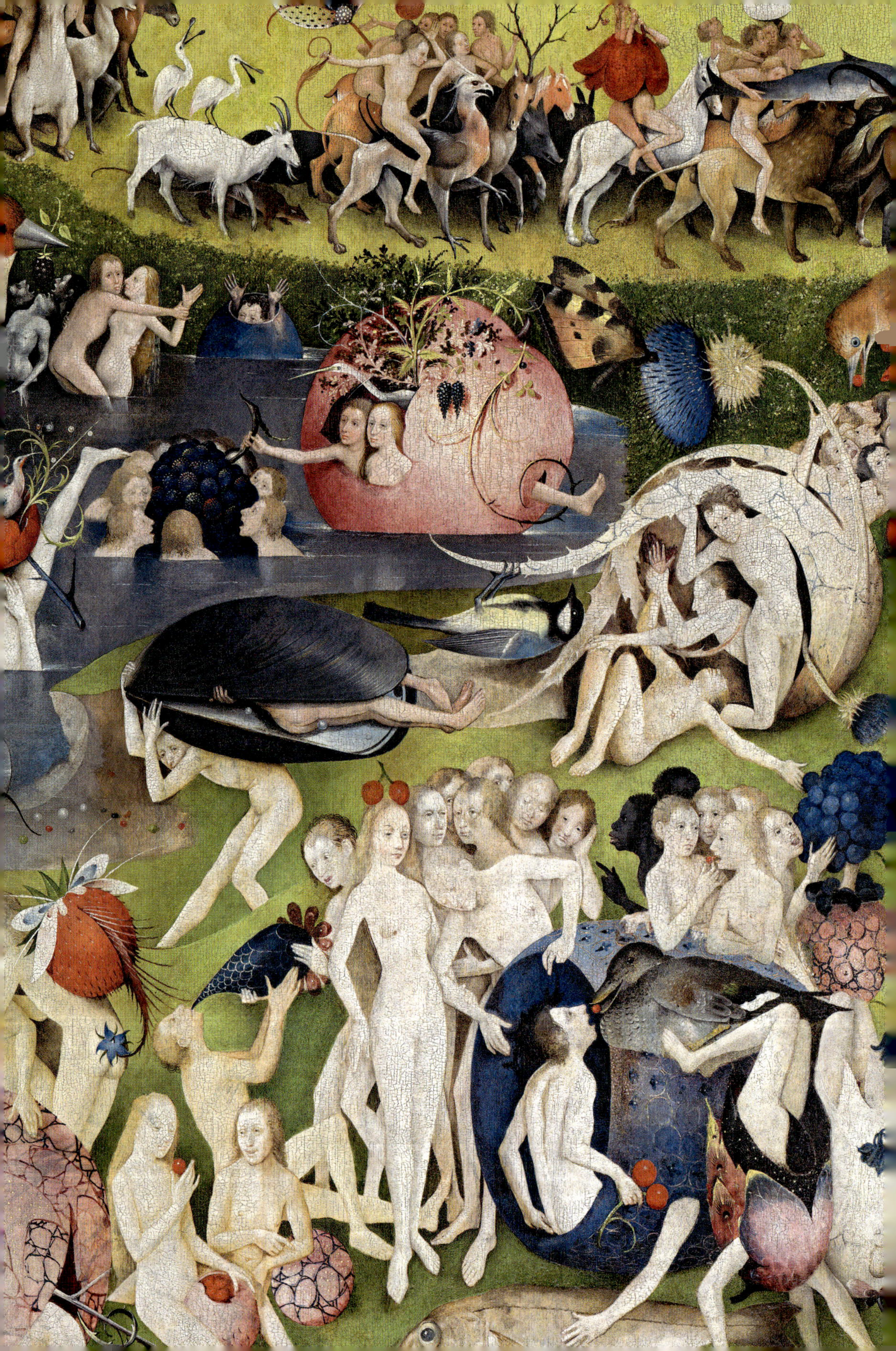

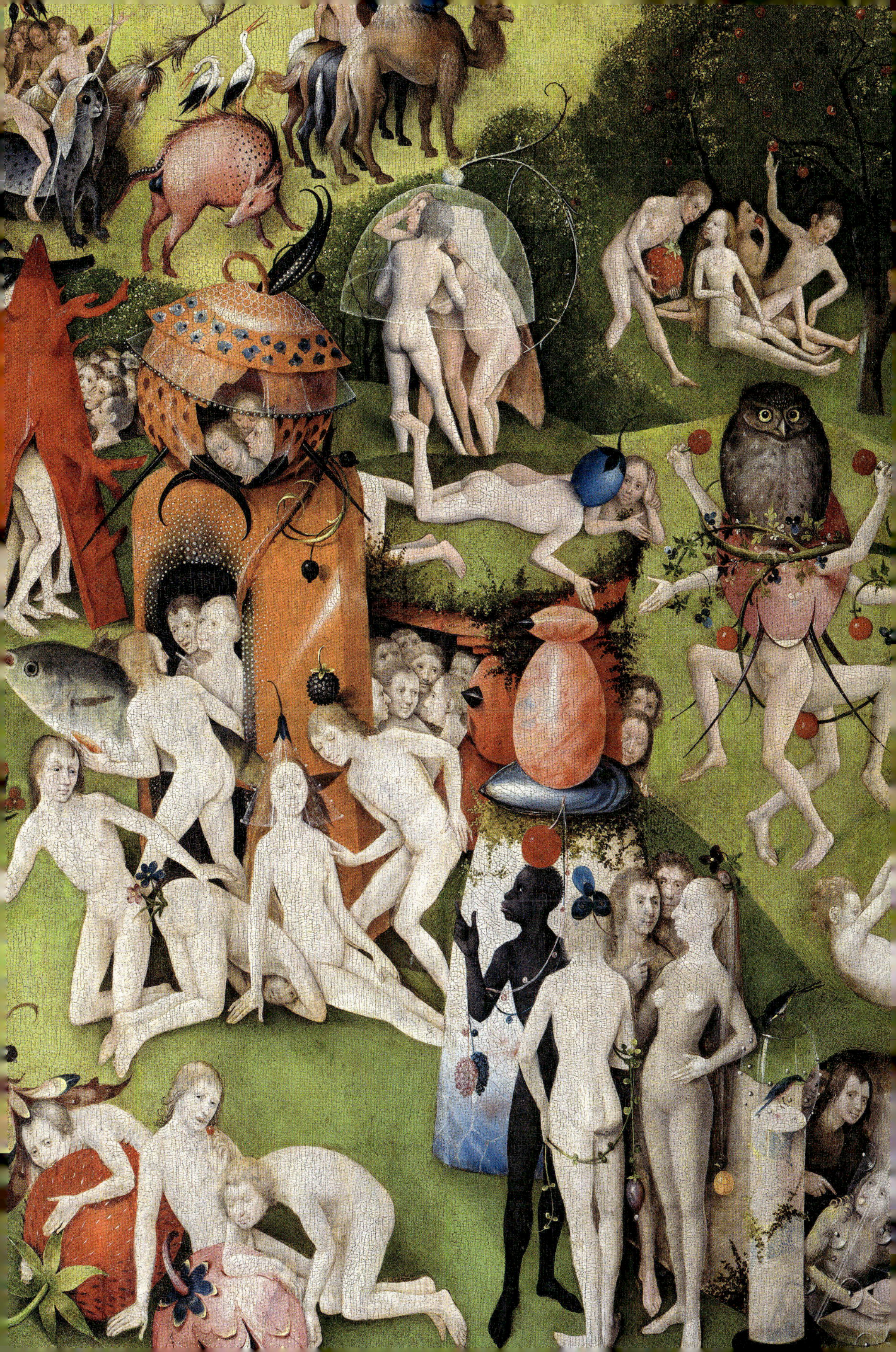

ALBRECHT DÜRER
1471–1528

The grass withers and the flowers fall,
because the breath of the Lord blows on them.
Surely the people are grass.

ISAIAH 40:7

In German artist Albrecht Dürer's engraving, we see an image of illicit love and life's impermanence. Two elaborately dressed lovers stroll through a rather eerie landscape. Art historians note the many symbols and allusions Dürer packed into this work – details that people of his day would have understood and used to interpret the work's meaning. Dürer gives his couple clothing to show the adulterous nature of their rendezvous. The young man's hat contains an ostrich feather, sign of a bachelor, while the woman's bonnet betrays her as being married. The man's roguish status is further emphasized by his fashionable shoes, more stylish than the pointed footwear of his companion, his somewhat aggressive gaze and the placement of his sword to resemble a rather enlarged phallus. Beyond the couple, peeking out from behind a barren tree, we see the image of Death in its most typical form: a skeleton. On Death's head balances an hourglass, another symbol of life's transience. Other death-related images may include the tall grassy plant below the man's outstretched hand, which historians suggest is related to biblical passages that compare the withering of plants to the wasting of human flesh. All in all, *The Promenade*'s message is a moral one – beware of wasting one's time with illicit pursuits, as life is short and death is always around the corner.

Copperplate engravings like *The Promenade* helped inspire a cultural revolution. The printing press was still a new invention in the late 1400s, and it enabled engravings and other printed images to become the first 'mass-produced' artworks. Dürer was not the first artist to make such prints, but he did more than anyone else to popularize them in the Renaissance. His expressive engravings spread his art – and his fame – around Europe with unprecedented speed. Soon, artists throughout the continent began creating prints of their own. It marked a first step in the process of democratizing fine art, making it available to more than just the wealthy elite.

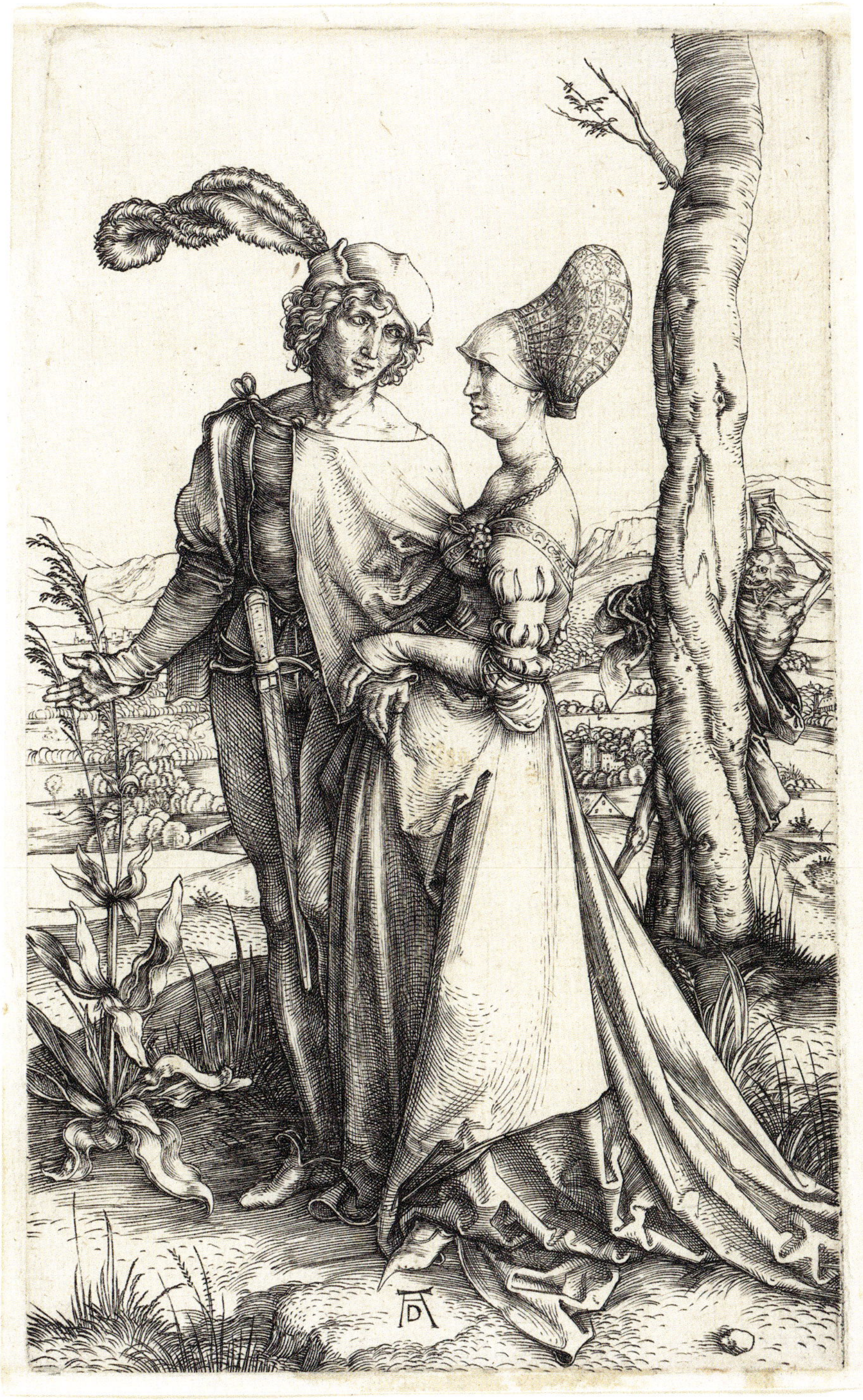

The Promenade (Death and the Lovers), c. 1498, engraving on laid paper,
19.5 × 12.1 cm (7 ⅝ × 4 ¾ in.), The Metropolitan Museum of Art, New York

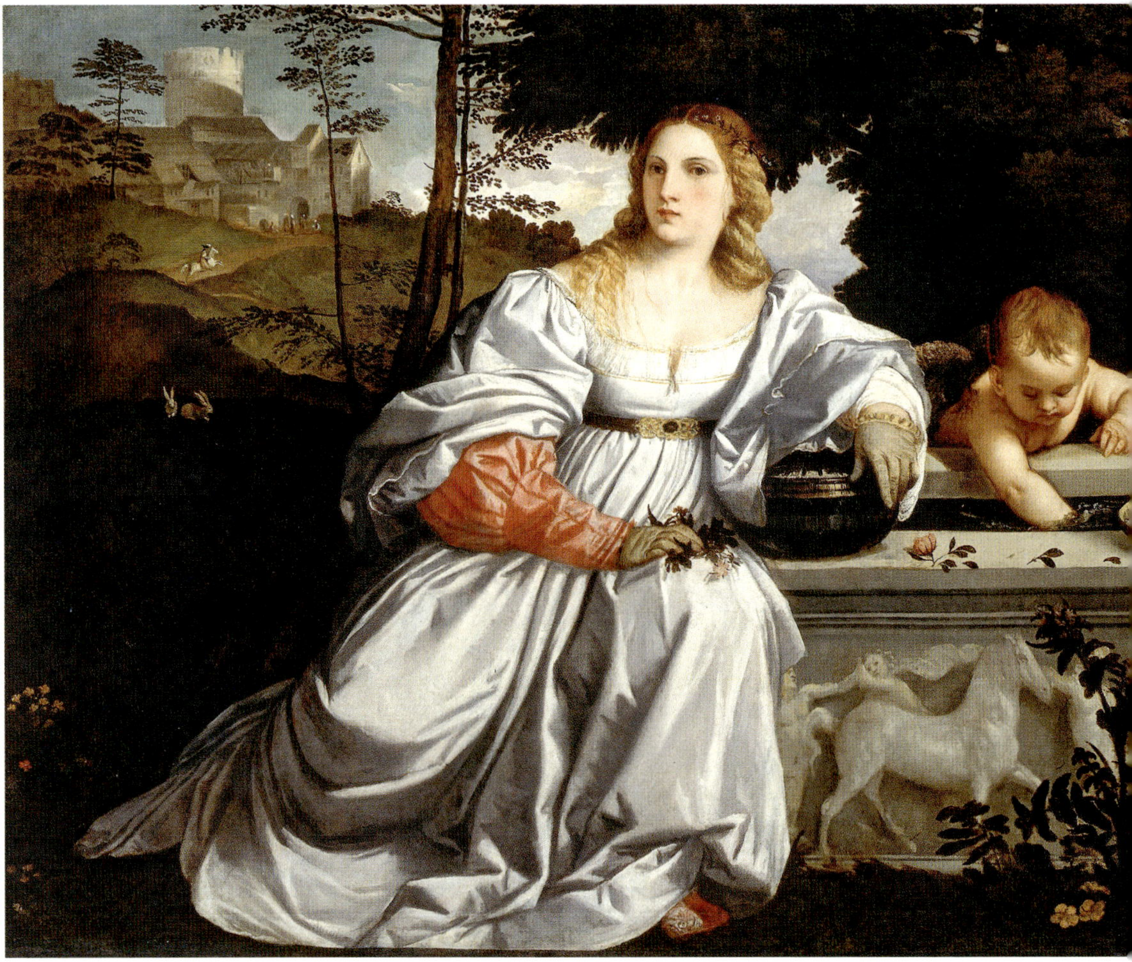

TITIAN
c. 1488/90–1576

To sum up, there are two aspects of Venus [...].
They are both accompanied by love.
[...] the first is impelled to contemplate the beauty of God,
and the second, to re-create this beauty in material forms.

MARSILIO FICINO, *ON LOVE: COMMENTARY ON PLATO'S SYMPOSIUM* (1469)

During the Renaissance, interest in the writings of Ancient Greece and Rome increased. Works of the Greek philosopher Plato (c. 428–c. 347 BC) became especially influential, and they inspired an entire philosophical movement now known as Neoplatonism. One aspect of Neoplatonism was its understanding of love. Renaissance authors like the Florentine Marsilio Ficino (1433–1499), through his interpretations of Plato's *Symposium*, argued that love could be understood by comparing the two 'aspects' of Venus (or Aphrodite in Greek). Venus, the goddess of beauty, inspires both material love (or love between man and woman) and celestial love (or love of God), and the two types of love should form a kind of union in our minds.

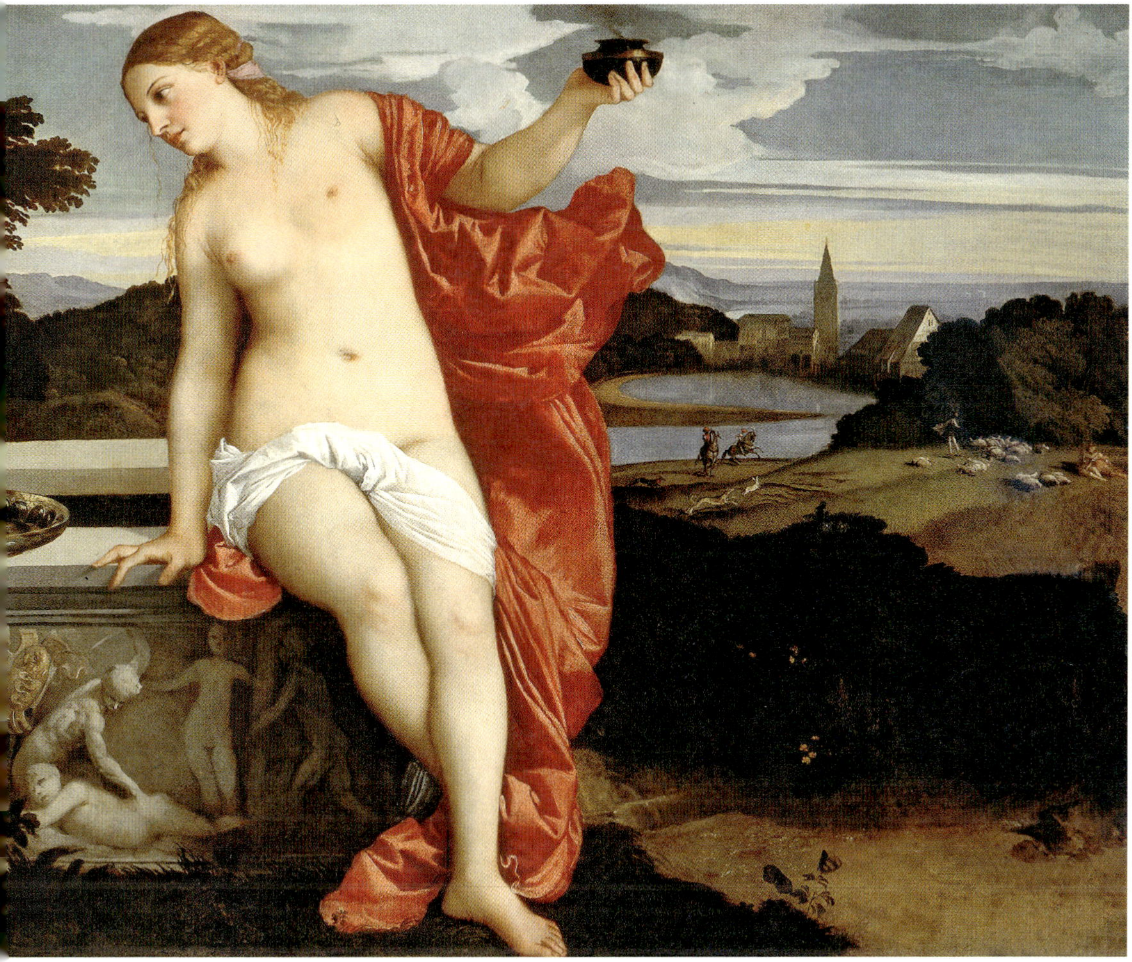

The philosophical ideas of Neoplatonism often made their way into paintings, which were nearly always created for the educated upper classes. One such 'Neoplatonic' painting may be *Sacred and Profane Love*, by Venetian Renaissance master Titian. Here we see two women, one elaborately clothed and one nude. Nude figures typically represented the divine nature of Venus, and this one is likely no exception. Moreover, the clothed woman's facial features resemble those of the nude, which has led some scholars to suggest she represents the other, earthly side of Venus. Other scholars argue that the clothed individual may simply be Titian's way of rendering earthly love through an 'ordinary' woman. But the artist's true intentions may never be known. The work did not even acquire its modern-day title until long after it was painted.

Despite these uncertainties, *Sacred and Profane Love* is one of Titian's most sumptuous paintings, displaying his mastery of colour and the human form, as well as his talent for landscape (as seen in the background). The canvas was likely painted for Niccolò Aurelio, a high-ranking official in the Venetian government – possibly to celebrate his marriage in 1514. Aurelio's family crest appears on the basin between the two female figures.

Sacred and Profane Love, 1514, oil on canvas,
118 × 278 cm (46 ½ × 109 ½ in.), Galleria Borghese, Rome

LUCAS CRANACH THE ELDER

c. 1472–1553

When the woman saw
that the fruit of the tree
was good for food and pleasing to the eye,
and also desirable for gaining wisdom,
she took some and ate it.
She also gave some to her husband,
who was with her, and he ate it.

GENESIS 3:6

Adam and Eve, who are banished from the Garden of Eden after eating God's forbidden fruit, mark the Bible's original tale of love and deception. Their story, however, did not become widespread in European art until the Renaissance – an age when the human body (and the natural world) were 'rediscovered' by painters and portrayed with unprecedented accuracy and detail. For some artists with large workshops, like that of German master Lucas Cranach the Elder, subjects such as Adam and Eve were painted multiple times for different clients. Cranach's own studio produced more than fifty versions of the story, the most impressive of which may be this version, now hanging at the Courtauld Gallery in London.

The Courtauld *Adam and Eve* displays much of what made Cranach's art distinctive. Like Sandro Botticelli, Cranach brilliantly combined realistic details, rich colour and elegant line, along with elements of fantasy and drama. The biblical couple is shown just before Adam takes a bite of the fruit. He appears uncertain, but Eve's face – with its rather seductive expression – suggests she will convince her partner to disobey God's command. Surrounding Adam and Eve are a menagerie of animals, including a lion, lamb, boar, stag and various birds. They are living peacefully together at the moment, but such harmony will soon be broken forever. Historians also note that Cranach includes both the serpent and a serpentine grape vine on the tree. The serpent represents deception and sin, while the vine is linked with Jesus's salvation: wine and grapes typically symbolize the blood Christ shed for humankind on the cross. Taken together, Cranach's expertly rendered images of nature reveal how God's love for His creation never dies, despite the disobedience of His human children.

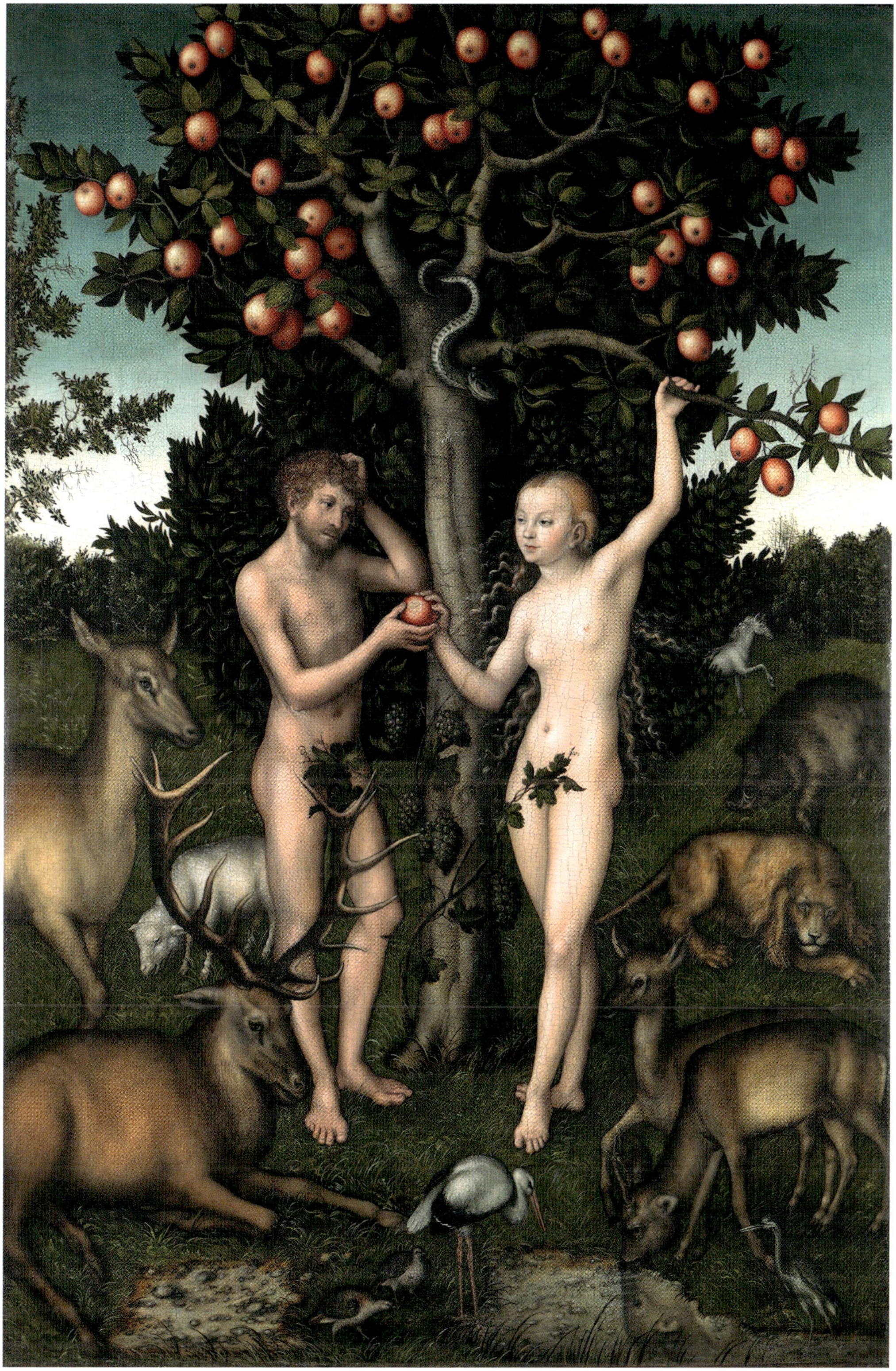

Adam and Eve, 1526, oil on panel,
117.1 × 80.8 cm (46 ⅛ × 31 ¾ in.), Courtauld Gallery, London

ANTONIO DA CORREGGIO
1489–1534

[Io] was already in flight.
She had left behind Lerna's pastures,
and the Lyrcean plain's wooded fields,
when the god [Jupiter] hid the wide earth in a covering of fog,
caught the fleeing girl, and raped her.

OVID, *METAMORPHOSES*, BOOK I (c. 1–8 AD)

In classical mythology, Io was the beautiful daughter of Inachus, king of the Greek city of Argos. Jupiter, the king of the gods and Roman equivalent of Zeus, was filled with lust for her and pursued her across the 'pastures' and 'fields' outside her city. Eventually, he disguised himself in a 'covering of fog', captured the terrified girl and had his way with her. Jupiter then tried to hide his misdeed from his wife, Juno, by transforming Io into a young cow, or heifer. But the disguise did not work, and Juno eventually discovered her husband's act of unfaithfulness – one of many he would inflict on her. At last, Io was transformed by Jupiter back into human form.

To modern readers, this bitter tale of lust, deception and sexual violence may seem repugnant, the opposite of true love. But for the ancient world, as well as the Renaissance, Jupiter's sexual exploits were understood as symbols of the creator god's power and authority. Such stories also inspired Renaissance artists to explore both the human form and the natural world. Italian painter Antonio da Correggio, who worked predominantly in Parma, portrayed the myth of Jupiter and Io in one of his finest works. Io is shown in an almost rapturous trance, as the arm of the god, covered in fog, wraps around her waist, and his barely visible face appears to kiss her cheek. This contrast between the gleaming pale skin of Io's body and Jupiter's ominous, misty form is striking. Correggio's powerfully erotic image departs from the traditional tale. Io's bearing is far from the frightened princess in Ovid's text; she seems to welcome – almost euphorically – Jupiter's advances. Erotic works like *Jupiter and Io* were relatively new in the early 1500s, a time when most Renaissance paintings had a more rigid, classical elegance. They would inspire a new generation of artists in the seventeenth century, during the Baroque age.

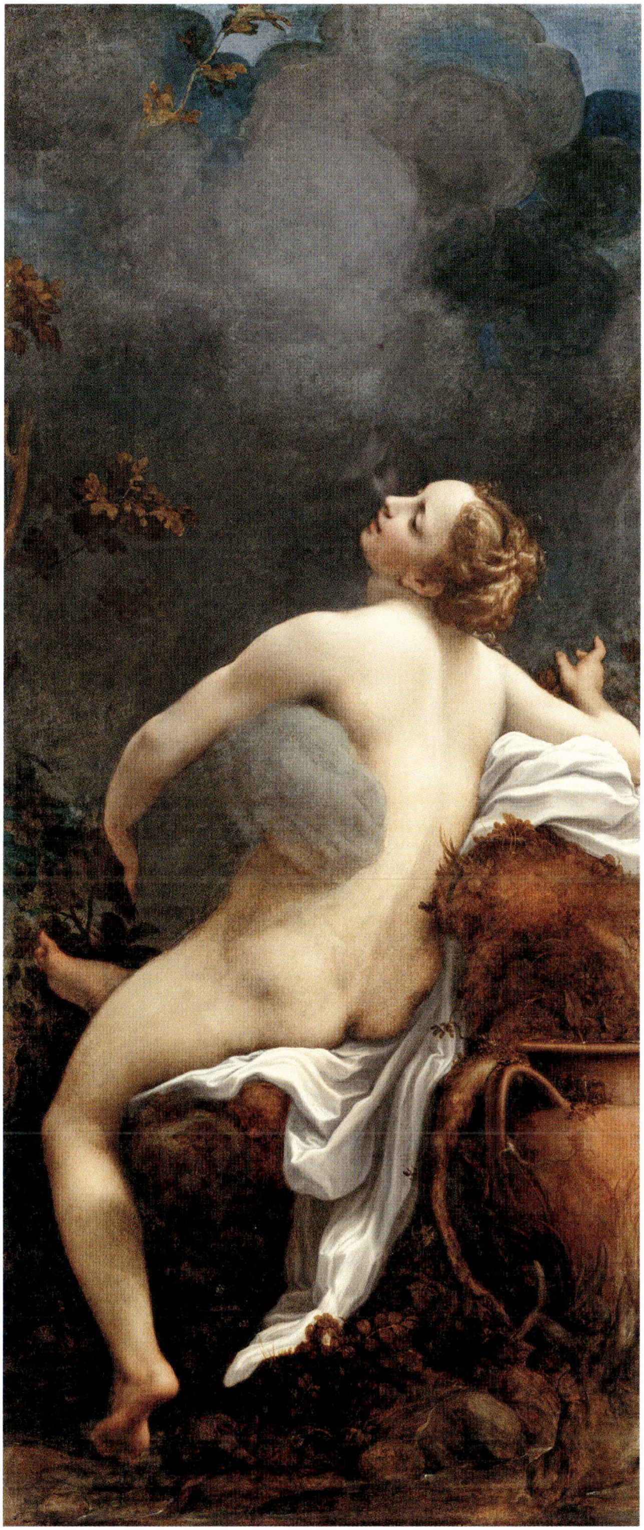

Jupiter and Io, c. 1530, oil on canvas,
162 × 73.5 cm (63 ¾ × 29 in.), Kunsthistorisches Museum, Vienna

AGNOLO BRONZINO
1503–1572

*And he [Bronzino] painted a picture of singular beauty
that was sent to King Francis in France,
wherein was a nude Venus, with a Cupid who was kissing her,
and Pleasure on one side with Play and other Loves,
and on the other side Fraud and Jealousy
and other passions of love.*

GIORGIO VASARI, *LIVES OF THE MOST EXCELLENT PAINTERS, SCULPTORS, AND ARCHITECTS*, VOL. III (1568)

In his biography of Agnolo Bronzino, Renaissance painter and historian Giorgio Vasari (1511–1574) described an enigmatic work the artist had painted for French King Francis I (1494–1547). Historians generally agree that this work is the one now held in London's National Gallery, even though there is no historical proof that the painting ever existed in the French royal collections. Like its history, the composition of the work is complex, defying and fascinating art critics for centuries. It has even led to confusion as to how the work should be titled: some call it *The Triumph of Venus*, while the National Gallery now names it *An Allegory with Venus and Cupid*.

Bronzino, the son of a butcher in Florence, rose through the ranks of Florentine society to become court painter for the powerful Medici family. He was especially famous for his elegant 'society' portraits, which depicted wealthy clients and their sumptuous clothing in exquisite detail. He was also a leading exponent of a late Renaissance style called Mannerism, a style well exemplified by *Allegory with Venus and Cupid*. Here the theme of love is presented as a dense, complicated allegory. Figures representing different aspects of love are crammed together to give the image an unsettling quality. Historians differ on the identity and meaning of all the figures, but the reclining woman in the centre is almost certainly Venus, the Roman goddess of sexual desire. Bronzino depicts her stretched across the foreground in a sensual pose, her lips almost touching those of winged Cupid to the immediate left. Cupid, who in ancient mythology is the son of Venus, is shown fondling his mother's breast; a remarkably sexualized detail set amidst other allegorical characters relating to earthly love. The bearded figure at top right likely represents Time, suggesting the need to enjoy life while one can; the putto (or nude child) with rose petals in his hand may symbolize Folly (or earthly pleasure); and the angry, open-mouthed male figure at far left possibly signifies Jealousy. But however one might analyse the details of this work, Bronzino's picture gives modern viewers a good understanding of the kind of art that appealed to wealthy clients in the Renaissance – art that required detailed knowledge of the ancient past, but that also catered to less lofty sexual desires.

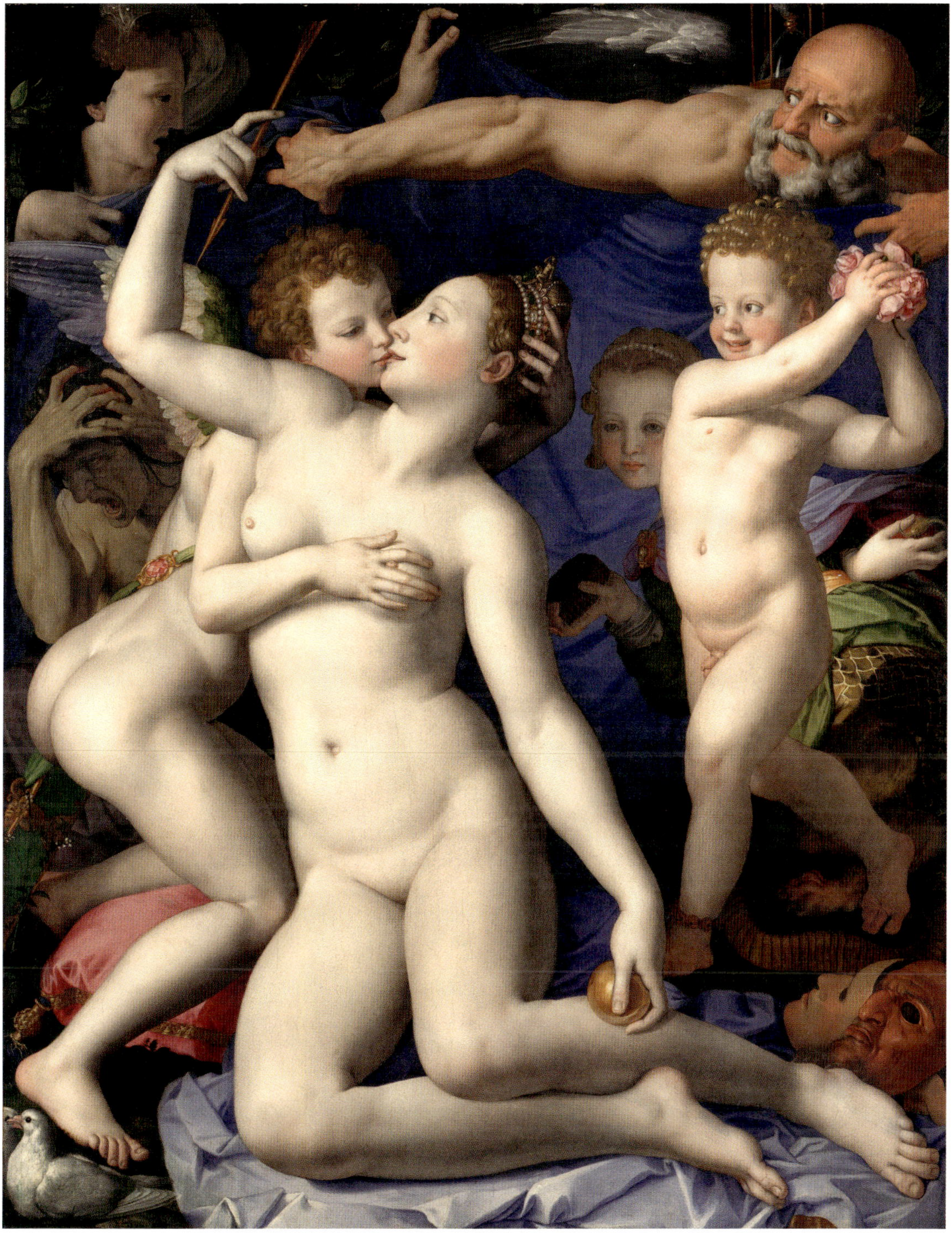

An Allegory with Venus and Cupid, c. 1545, oil on panel,
146.1 × 116.2 cm (57 ½ × 45 ¾ in.), The National Gallery, London

PIETER BRUEGEL THE ELDER

c. 1525/30–1569

*They marry their children into strange towns,
yea and foreign countries,
and marry noble with ignoble,
young with old, master
and servant, which is not commendable.*

LODOVICO GUICCIARDINI, *DESCRIPTION OF ALL THE LOW COUNTRIES* (1567)

For much of European history, elaborate marriage ceremonies were reserved for the wealthy – while peasants often became 'man and wife' merely by choosing to live together. This state of affairs began to change in the sixteenth century. Peasants in the Low Countries (which make up present-day Belgium and the Netherlands) had become relatively prosperous. They had won their freedom from feudal lords and could enjoy the wealth of their own labours. Italian writer Lodovico Guicciardini (1521–1589) settled in Flanders and travelled through northern Europe. In his *Description of All the Low Countries* (1567), he not only wrote about the wines and agricultural products of this region, but also the industriousness of its people and the occasional custom of marriages between social classes. Such marriages were often lively, boisterous affairs, and few artists of the age portrayed them with as much flair as Flemish painter Pieter Bruegel the Elder.

Bruegel's *Peasant Wedding* is a joyous tribute to rural prosperity. The barn in which the wedding is held proudly displays sheaves of wheat on the wall, a sign not only of a good harvest but of hoped for fertility in the union. The picture also shows a compelling mix of rich and poor. One of the servants carrying the *rijstpap* (or pudding) has a spoon in his hat – an indication that he is poor and must bring his own utensil with him when begging for food. Yet he stands in front of a well-dressed, bearded man whom scholars believe may be a wealthy landlord. Next to the servants and the landlord sit numerous farmers who are simply enjoying their beer and food.

One person who is not allowed to drink at the wedding is the bride. She sits in front of a celebratory green cloth hanging on the wall and wears a paper crown. A serene figure with hands clasped, she is a model of feminine virtue. Historians are unsure which of the figures is the groom. He may be the man at left filling jugs for the guests, or he may be the man in the dark coat at the centre of the composition. But unresolved questions aside, *Peasant Wedding* remains a vivid, unvarnished glimpse of communal celebration during the Renaissance.

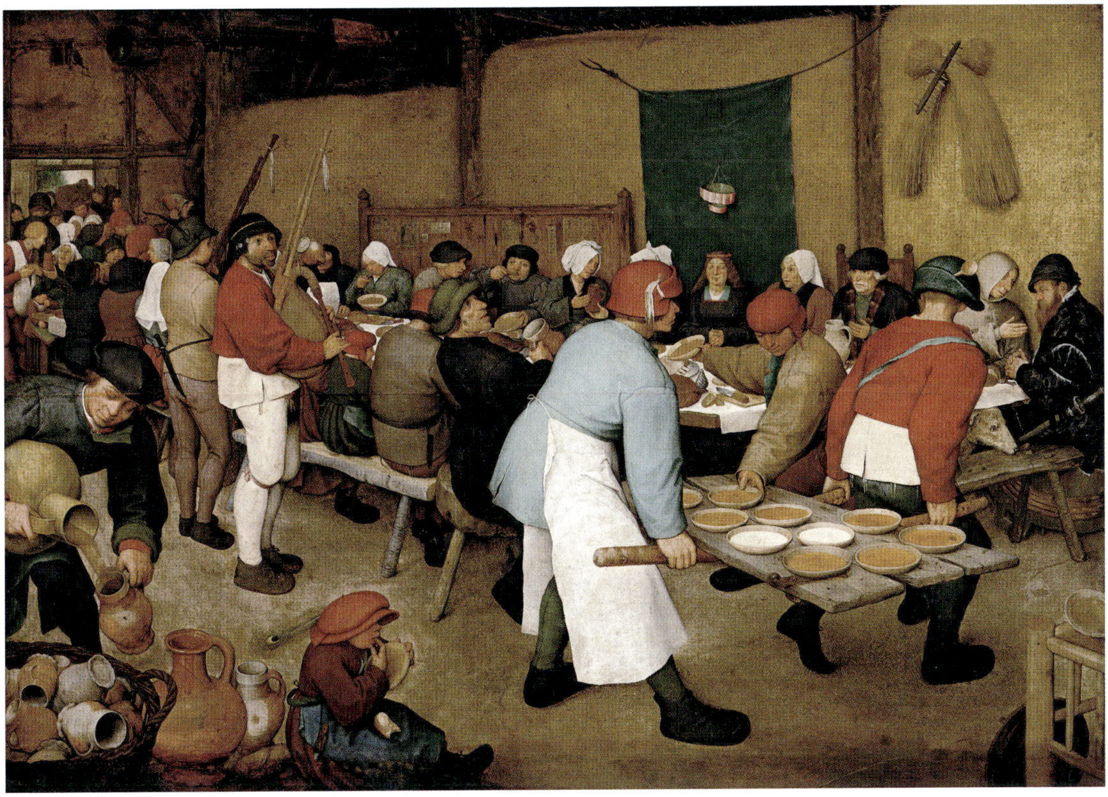

Peasant Wedding, c. 1567, oil on oak panel,
113 × 164 cm (44 ½ × 64 ⅝ in.), Kunsthistorisches Museum, Vienna

CARAVAGGIO
1571–1610

How often he gave his lips in vain to the deceptive pool,
how often, trying to embrace the neck he could see,
he plunged his arms into the water,
but could not catch himself within them!
What he has seen he does not understand,
but what he sees he is on fire for,
and the same error both seduces and deceives his eyes.

OVID, *METAMORPHOSES* (c. 1–8 AD), BOOK III

In his *Metamorphoses*, ancient Roman poet Ovid (43 BC–AD 17/18) wrote of the mythical hunter Narcissus, who spurned offers of love from women only to fall in love with his own reflection in a pool. But this form of love, of course, proved to be unrequited. When Narcissus tried to embrace his own reflection in the pool, the image became obscured and disappeared. The young man cried out, 'Where do you fly to? Stay, cruel one, do not abandon one who loves you! I am allowed to gaze at what I cannot touch, and so provide food for my miserable passion!' But his cries went unheard by his reflection. Distraught, Narcissus became 'weakened and melted' by love, and his body eventually transformed into a flower with 'white petals surrounding a yellow heart'.

Ovid's tale of Narcissus was especially admired by Italian poets and artists of the Renaissance and Baroque eras. The renowned Italian painter Caravaggio created his own version in the late 1590s. Caravaggio had developed a distinctive, highly influential style that often-featured individuals set dramatically against a darkened background. Piercing light, usually shown emanating from the left of the canvas, illuminates his figures. The artist also used deep chiaroscuro (or strong contrasts between light and shade) to model skin and clothing, features he typically presented in a gritty, naturalistic manner. Many of these techniques can be seen in *Narcissus*. The young man appears almost nothing like a figure from classical mythology. He is depicted as an ordinary Roman of Caravaggio's time, with rumpled clothes and slightly grimy hands and face. The 'pool' in which he finds his reflection looks rather like a dirty street puddle, and the reflection itself – almost obscured in darkness – is anything but classically romantic. Caravaggio's *Narcissus* is an ominous warning of the dangers of self-love, without any hint of the narcissus flowers promised by Ovid.

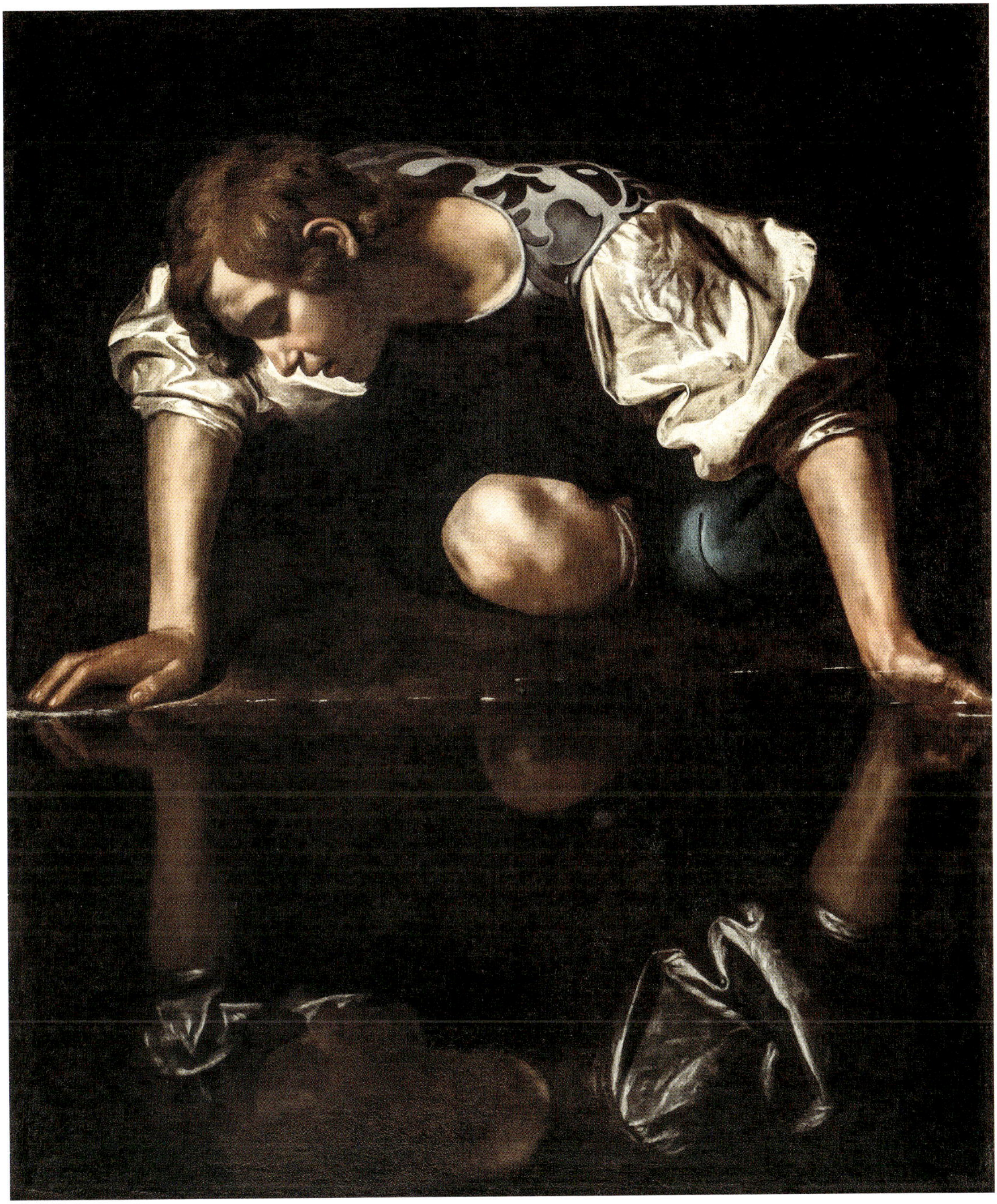

Narcissus, c. 1597–1598, oil on canvas,
113.3 × 97 cm (44 ⅝ × 38 ⅛ in.), Galleria Nazionale d'Arte Antica, Rome

PETER PAUL RUBENS
1577–1640

She had no capricious moods,
and no feminine weakness,
but was all goodness and honesty.
And because of her virtues
she was loved during her lifetime [...]

PETER PAUL RUBENS ON HIS LATE WIFE, ISABELLA BRANT,
FROM A LETTER TO PIERRE DUPUY (1626)

On 3 October 1609, Flemish artist Peter Paul Rubens married Isabella Brant, the teenaged daughter of a wealthy government official in Antwerp. Their marriage would prove a happy one, with Isabella giving birth to three children before she died in 1626. The couple's affection is reflected in this grand double portrait Rubens painted to commemorate their wedding. Following the tradition of other artists of his day, Rubens included many symbolic details in the work. His choice of setting, for example, is a bower or grove of honeysuckle bushes. The honeysuckle flower symbolized endurance and steadfastness, a wish for their union to be a lasting one. In addition, the couple is shown holding each other's right hands, indicating a union of equals.

Rubens was a thirty-two-year-old artist on the rise in 1609. He had travelled throughout Italy and received important commissions in Genoa, Mantua and Rome, and was received at the Spanish court in Madrid. He had subsequently become an official court painter at Brussels. These early successes would lead to a dazzling career as a prized artist in royal houses throughout Europe. One can already see Rubens's ambition in *The Honeysuckle Bower*, as the painter depicts himself and his wife adorned in the finest silks, laced collars, brocaded fabrics and jewellery – as well as the aristocratic sword he holds in his left hand. Yet despite all of this finery, the couple's facial expressions and postures have a casual air; the look of a man and wife enjoying their day together in the country. With its combination of formality and relaxed charm, *Rubens and Isabella Brant in the Honeysuckle Bower* remains one of the most distinctive and joyous images of married love.

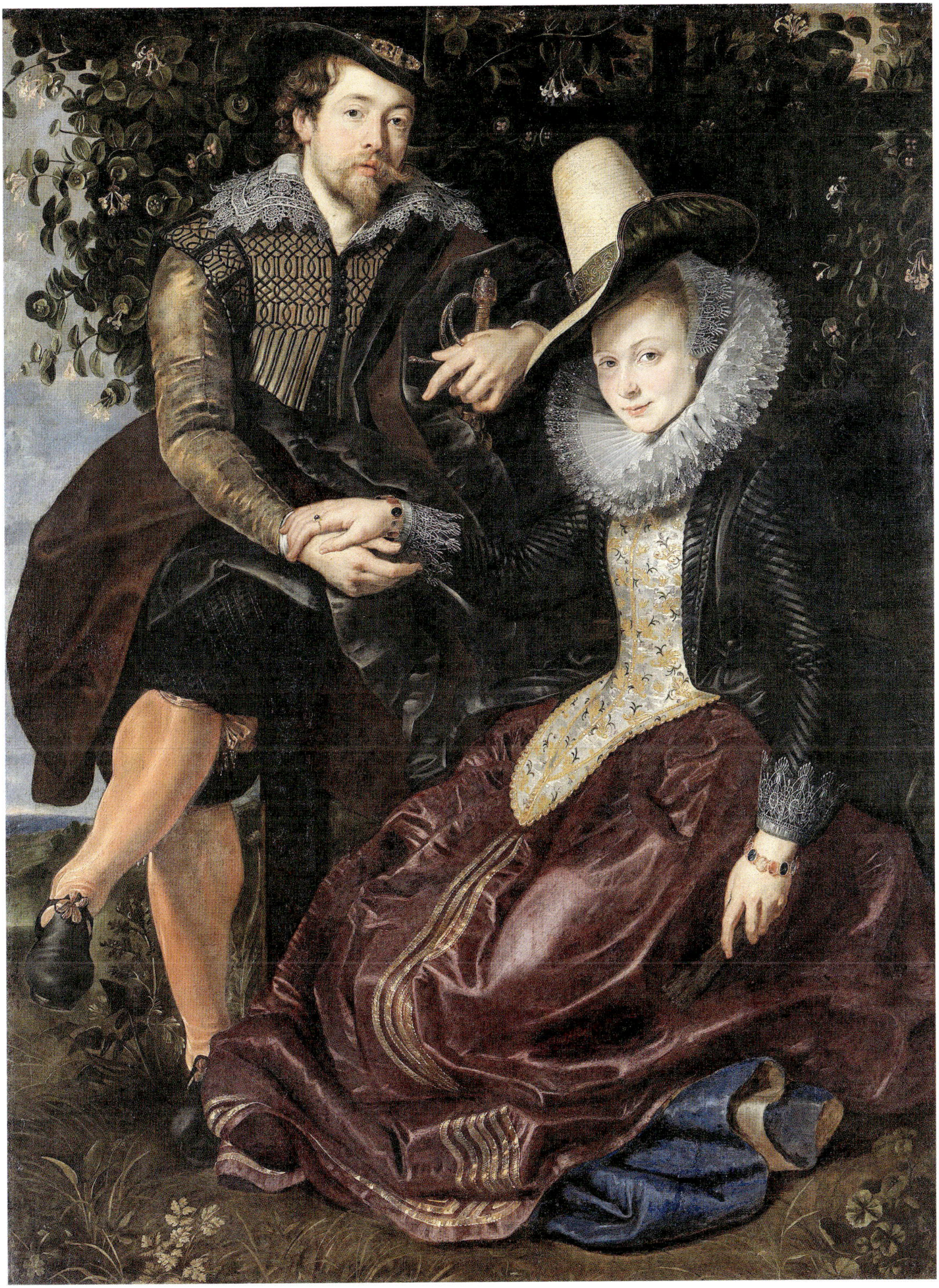

Rubens and Isabella Brant in the Honeysuckle Bower, c. 1609/10, oil on canvas,
178 × 136.5 cm (70 ⅛ × 53 ¾ in.), Bayerische Staatsgemäldesammlungen – Alte Pinakothek, Munich

ARTEMISIA GENTILESCHI

1593–1654 or later

*Then she [Delilah] said to him [Samson], '
How can you say, "I love you", when you won't confide in me?'
[...] So he told her everything.
'No razor has ever been used on my head',
he said, [...] 'If my head were shaved,
my strength would leave me,
and I would become as weak as any other man.'*

JUDGES 16:15–17

In the biblical Book of Judges we find the heroic tale of Samson, the Nazirite warrior whose strength could overpower any other man. But Samson's fate was sealed when he fell in love with a woman named Delilah, who tricked him into telling her the secret of his powers – his beautiful hair. She then put him 'to sleep on her lap' and had the 'seven braids of his hair' cut off. Now powerless, Samson was captured by the enemy Philistine army, who gouged out his eyes and imprisoned him. Samson would later regain enough of his hair (and his strength) to destroy the Philistine temple, but he would sacrifice his own life in the process.

Samson's story offers a timeless warning about the dangers of 'love at first sight' – the way it can make a person vulnerable and, in Samson's case, subject to mortal threat. It became a popular subject for artists of the Renaissance and Baroque periods. Painters including Peter Paul Rubens used the Samson character to display their talent for portraying heroic, muscular flesh. But other artists offered more subtle interpretations of the story.

Artemisia Gentileschi was the most successful female painter of the seventeenth century. Trained by her father, Orazio (1563–1639), she produced art for princely families throughout Italy, as well as King Charles I of England. She also became the first woman admitted into Florence's prestigious Accademia delle Arti del Disegno (Academy of the Arts of Drawing). Artemisia's style, like that of Caravaggio, featured dramatically lit scenes set against dark backgrounds. Focusing on the exploits of women in the Bible, she created images of female bravery and agency. Her *Samson and Delilah*, for example, shows Delilah holding the scissors she will use to cut off Samson's hair. This detail departs from the biblical text, which says she 'called for someone' to perform the act. As a result, Artemisia's Delilah becomes a stronger, more active protagonist in this ancient tale of love and deception.

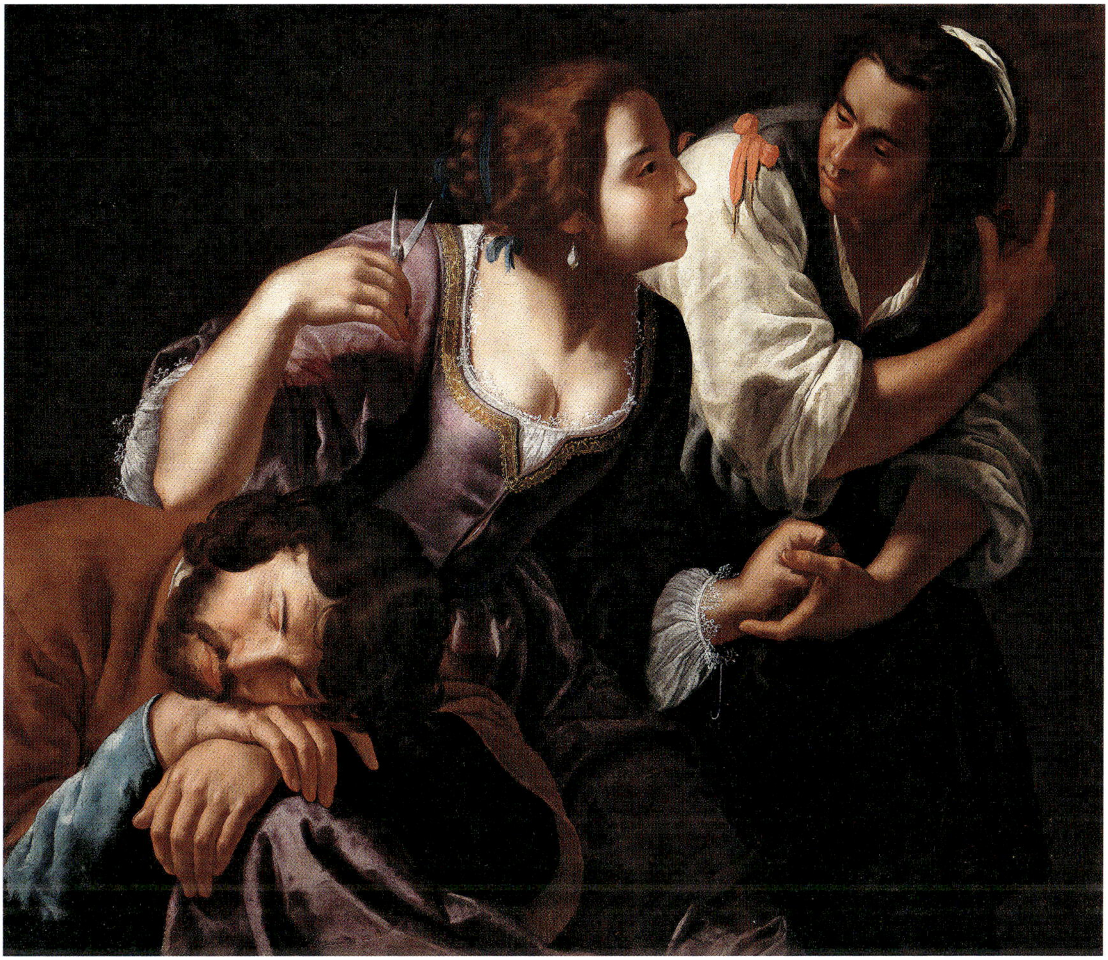

Samson and Delilah, c. 1630, oil on canvas,
90.5 × 109.5 cm (35 ⅝ × 43 ⅛ in.), Gallerie d'Italia, Palazzo del Banco di Napoli, Naples

JOHANNES VERMEER

1632–1675

With the recovery of the Cupid in the background [...] the actual intention of the Delft painter becomes apparent [...] it is a fundamental statement about the essence of true love.

STEPHAN KOJA, DIRECTOR OF THE GEMÄLDEGALERIE ALTE MEISTER, DRESDEN (2021)

In 2017, art historians at the Gemäldegalerie Alte Meister in Dresden, Germany, were analysing one of the museum's most famous paintings, *Girl Reading a Letter at an Open Window* by Dutch master Johannes Vermeer. The painting had long been admired for its subtle depiction of light, which pours through a window at the left and illuminates the scene. The work also shows Vermeer's mastery of painted textures, such as the shimmering, richly coloured tapestry, the woman's glossy silk bodice and the muted reflections in the glass of the open window. All of these textures were achieved using expertly placed patches and daubs of paint. In addition, the woman depicted has a slightly melancholy, lovelorn aura about her, imbuing the work with a sense of mystery.

But what the German researchers discovered in 2017 surprised them. Using X-ray analysis, they found that the back wall of the young woman's room, which had long appeared blank, was significantly repainted after Vermeer's death. The imaging revealed what appeared to be a large, framed picture of Cupid that Vermeer had originally included as part of the background. Over the next four years, restorers carefully scraped away the overpaint and restored Vermeer's image of Cupid – revealing for the first time in centuries how the painter intended his work to look.

Stephan Koja, then Director of the Dresden museum, along with other art historians, now believe *Girl Reading a Letter at an Open Window* is a direct visual metaphor of love. The wistful, isolated girl may in fact be reading a love letter from a distant suitor. Above her, the watchful figure of Cupid once again stares out directly at the viewer, an invitation to contemplate the scene and its message.

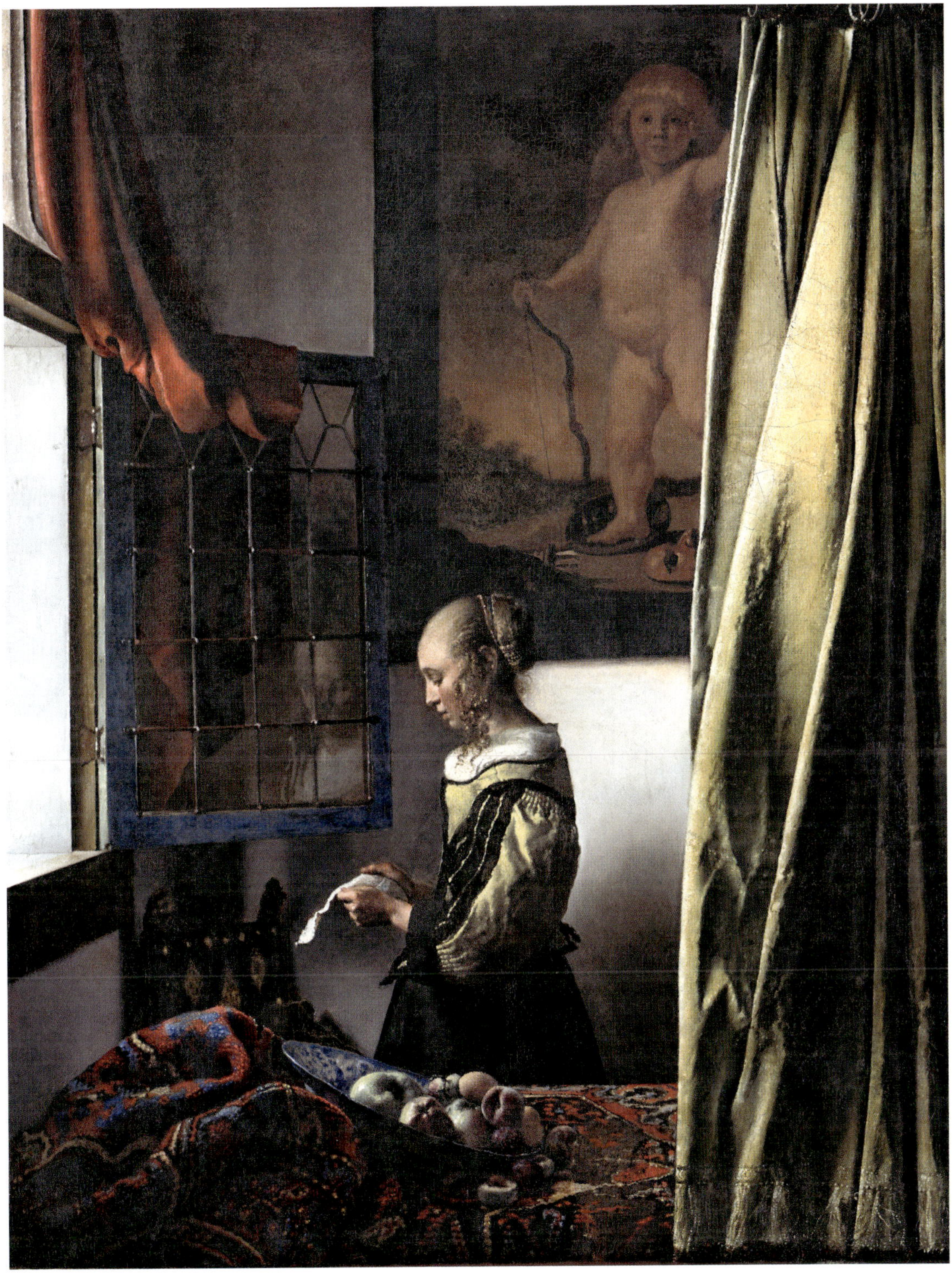

Girl Reading a Letter at an Open Window, c. 1657–1659, oil on canvas,
83 × 64.5 cm (32 ⅝ × 25 ⅜ in.), Gemäldegalerie Alte Meister, Staatliche Kunstsammlungen Dresden

ANTOINE WATTEAU
1684–1721

The great poet of the eighteenth century is Watteau. [...]
The painter drew enchanting visions
from the depths of his fantasy, an ideal world.
Beyond the limits of his own time
he constructed one of those Shakespearean kingdoms,
one of those lands which are light
and filled with love [...]

EDMOND AND JULES DE GONCOURT,
ART OF THE EIGHTEENTH CENTURY (1859–1875)

With his charming scenes, or *fêtes galantes* (courtship parties), French painter Antoine Watteau set a new trend in the way love could be depicted on canvas. These images, often inspired by the French and Italian theatre of his day, have a dreamlike quality to them, with characters that appear more as actors in a romantic drama than as real people.

Watteau's *Pilgrimage to the Isle of Cythera*, historically titled *The Embarkation for Cythera*, was created as a presentation piece to mark his acceptance to France's Royal Academy of Painting and Sculpture. Membership in the academy gave French artists of the day a higher status, as well as greater access to wealthy clients in Paris. The painting shows us a group of pilgrims on their way to Cythera, the Greek island famous as the home of Venus, Roman goddess of love. Watteau chose this theme, in part, because he knew the Academy preferred works with 'historical' themes to those featuring contemporary life. For eighteenth-century France, the 'history' painter was considered the most distinguished type of artist, one who could use his powers of invention to recreate important moments of the past. Painting modern life, in contrast, was considered facile and vulgar, the work of common craftsmen rather than true artists.

Despite its references to the classical past, *Pilgrimage to the Isle of Cythera* is far from a stiff, academic work. Watteau's pilgrims, attired in contemporary eighteenth-century dress, are arranged as a series of couples, each of whom carries out a different romantic gesture. One woman is being assisted off the ground by her lover, another holds a fan while listening to an amorous speech, while other couples process elegantly arm in arm. All of these vignettes could have been witnessed in a garden at Versailles, or on a Parisian stage. But Watteau sets his figures against a vast, misty landscape, which acts as the main 'character' in the painting. His people seem almost dwarfed in this 'Shakespearean kingdom', giving the image an uneasy, somewhat melancholy undertone. The atmosphere is enhanced by a sculptural image of Venus, shown as a ruined legless herm, its arms now missing, seemingly dissolving into the wooded landscape, as well as by chubby putti flying off into the distance. For many, Watteau's composition suggests the transitory nature of love, an idyllic emotion that is always slightly out of reach.

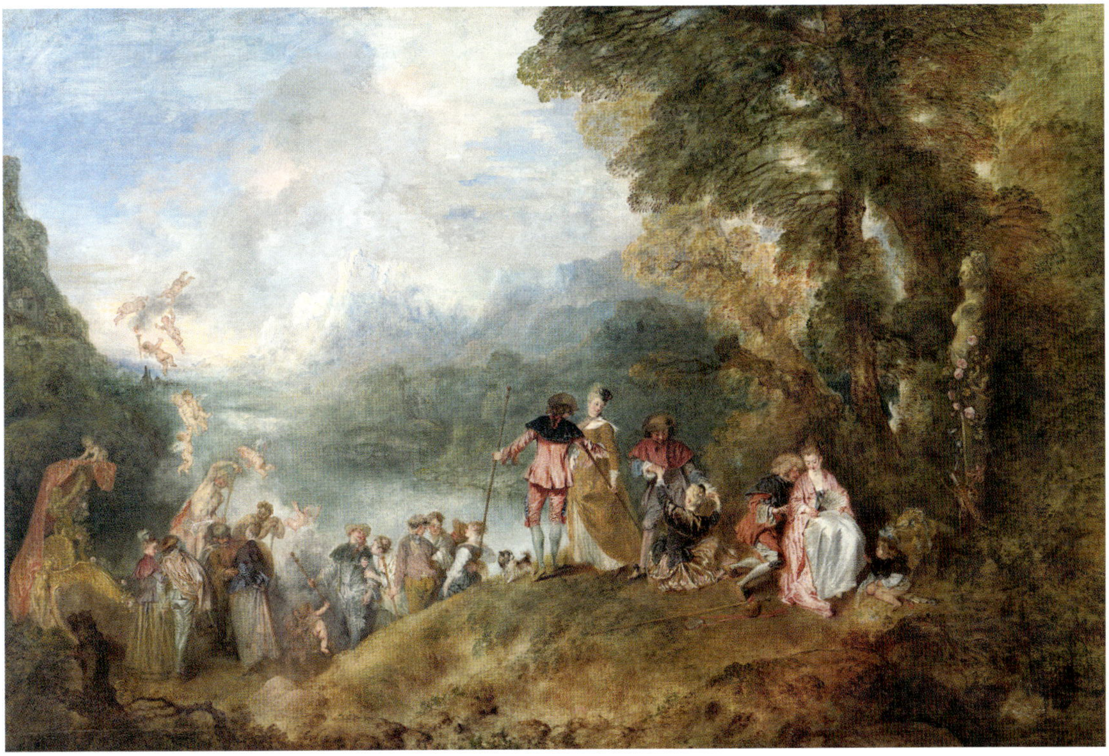

Pilgrimage to the Isle of Cythera, 1717, oil on canvas,
129 × 194 cm (50 ¾ × 76 ⅜ in.), Musée du Louvre, Paris

THE KOTA MASTER

early 18th century

Lord Krishna dragged her [Radha] to his breast
and kissed her lips (upper and lower),
the chin and both sides of her cheek.
Radha also kissed the handsome lunar face of Krishna
and with both her hands pressed Krishna,
the Lord of her life, to her bosom.

BRAHMA VAIVARTA PURANA
(c. 15TH–16TH CENTURY), CHAPTER 127

Sacred Hindu texts tell of Krishna, the god of protection and love, and his partner Radha, goddess of love and devotion. Together they inhabit Goloka, an eternal, celestial world of cows and other symbols of divinity. Some Hindu traditions refer to Krishna and Radha as a married couple, while others speak of Radha as a chief consort or lover. But for most Hindus, Radha and Krishna are commonly worshipped as the ideal form of love between man and woman. Artists, in fact, have presented the two gods as a single being, Radha-Krishna, with Radha taking up the left side of Krishna's body – a representation of the combined masculine and feminine attributes of divinity.

The sacred Sanskrit text known as the *Brahma Vaivarta Purana* describes Radha and Krishna's lovemaking in sensual detail; and many artists over the centuries have created lush images of the godly couple. The illustrated page shown here, which dates from the early 1700s, depicts Radha and Krishna in a vivid world reminiscent of Goloka with fanciful trees and flowers, long-necked peacocks and an intense orange and blue sky. The bodies of Krishna, with his traditional blue skin, and the pink-skinned Radha are interlocked as one, with their eyes focused intensely on each other as they stroll through their blessed world. The unnamed artist, who clothes his deities in garments typical of eighteenth-century Indian nobility, is known today only as the Kota Master. He lived during a time when nearly all of the Indian subcontinent was part of the Mughal Empire, governed by a Muslim dynasty that tolerated the Hindu faith.

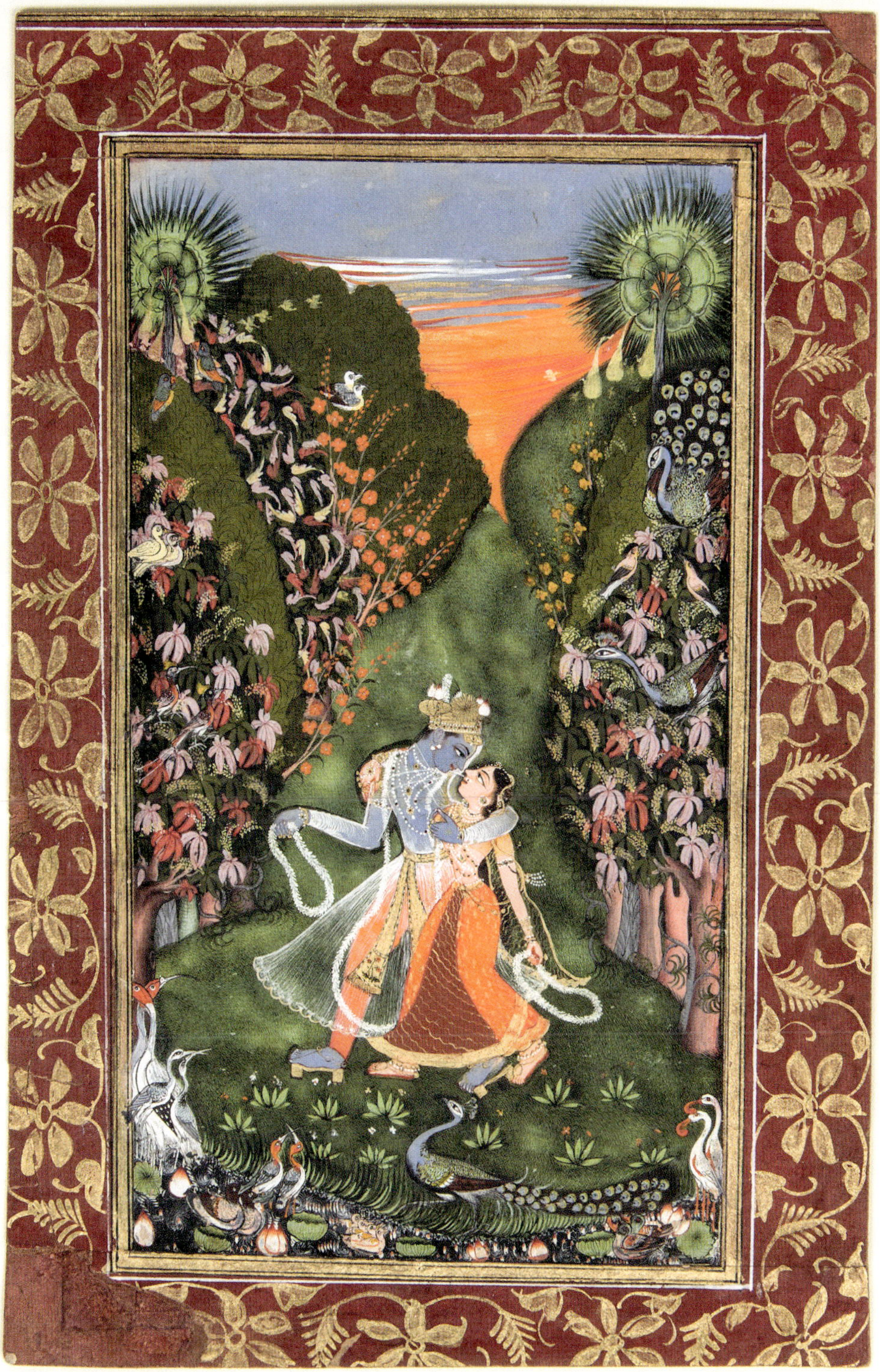

Radha and Krishna Walk in a Flowering Grove, c. 1720, ink, opaque watercolour and gold on paper, 19.1 × 11.1 cm (7 ½ × 4 ⅜ in.), The Metropolitan Museum of Art, New York

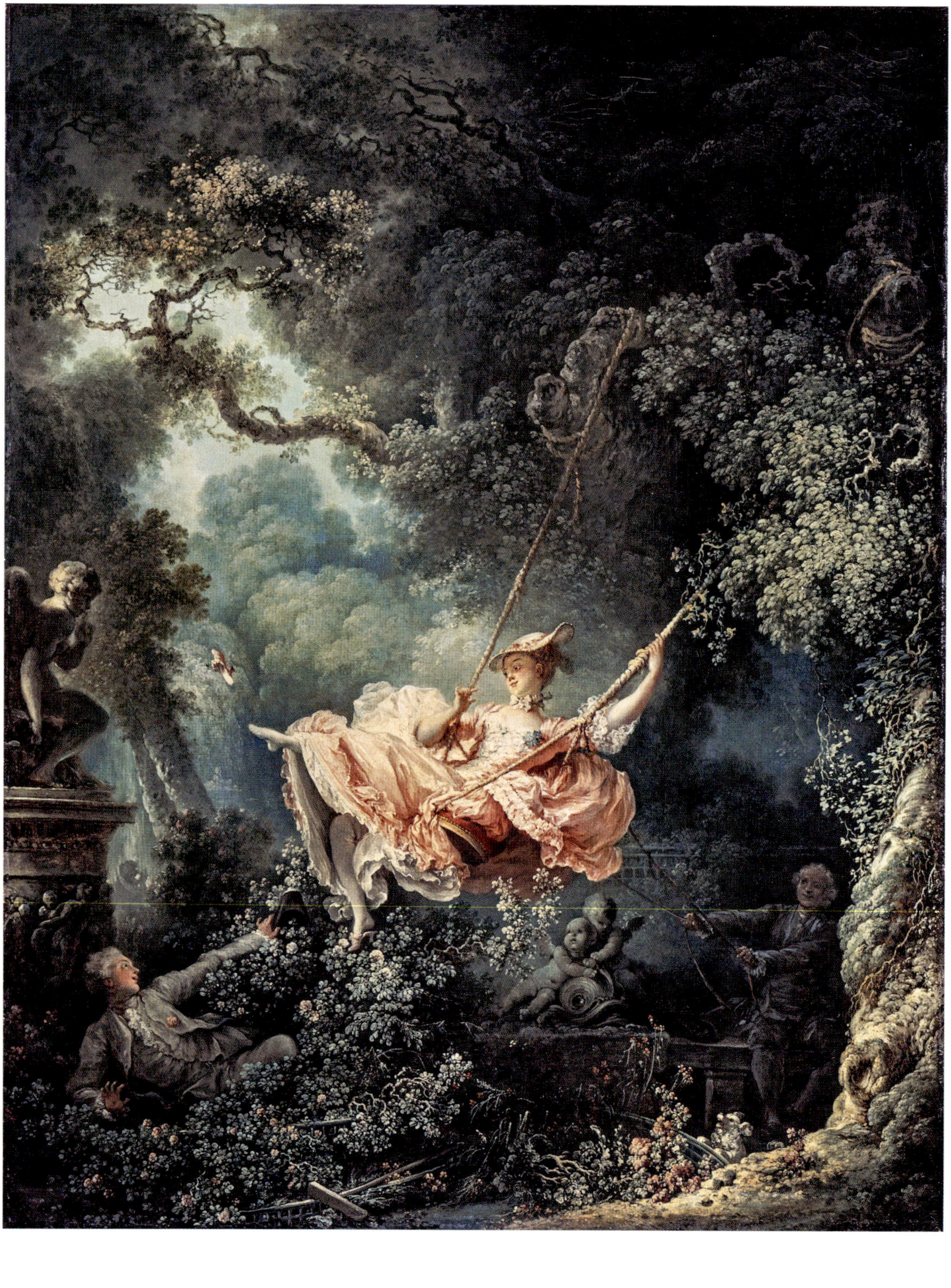

The Swing, c. 1767/68, oil on canvas,
81 × 64.2 cm (31 ⅞ × 25 ¼ in.), The Wallace Collection, London

JEAN-HONORÉ FRAGONARD

1732–1806

I should like to have you paint Madame [pointing to his mistress] on a swing that a bishop would push. You will place me in such a way that I would be able to see the legs of this lovely girl [...]

FROM CHARLES COLLÉ'S JOURNAL (1767), RECOUNTING HOW AN UNNAMED COURTIER ATTEMPTED TO COMMISSION GABRIEL-FRANÇOIS DOYEN TO PAINT *THE SWING*

Jean-Antoine Watteau's *Pilgrimage to the Isle of Cythera* (p. 51) helped inspire an art movement known as Rococo. Painters around Europe began depicting their own *fêtes galantes* (courtship parties) for an array of wealthy and royal patrons. Rococo art featured the graceful figures and romantic scenes of nature found in Watteau but without the earlier artist's emotional depth. Watteau's subtle feelings of melancholy were replaced with images of pure frivolity.

The charming scene shown here, today known simply as *The Swing*, was painted by French artist Jean-Honoré Fragonard. The work was made for an unknown nobleman, long thought to be François-David Bollioud de Saint-Julien (1713–1788), a baron and wealthy tax farmer for the French clergy. This aristocrat had originally commissioned Gabriel-François Doyen (1726–1806) to paint the work. But Doyen, an academic painter of historical and biblical scenes, felt the subject beneath him and refused. Eventually, Fragonard agreed to the courtier's eccentric terms, and the work was completed in the late 1760s.

In many ways, *The Swing* perfectly captures the mood of aristocratic Europe before the French Revolution. It was an age when elites isolated themselves from the problems of poverty and unrest among ordinary people and created closed-off worlds of fantasy where they could enjoy the pleasures of life without guilt. Fragonard's fancifully dressed woman casually flips her shoe in the air as her lover adoringly gazes up at her from below a statue of Cupid. It is a purely theatrical vision of love, one that intentionally avoids emotional subtlety. Today, the work is admired for Fragonard's technical brilliance as an artist, his ability to create people and objects that seem to dance and move to their own music.

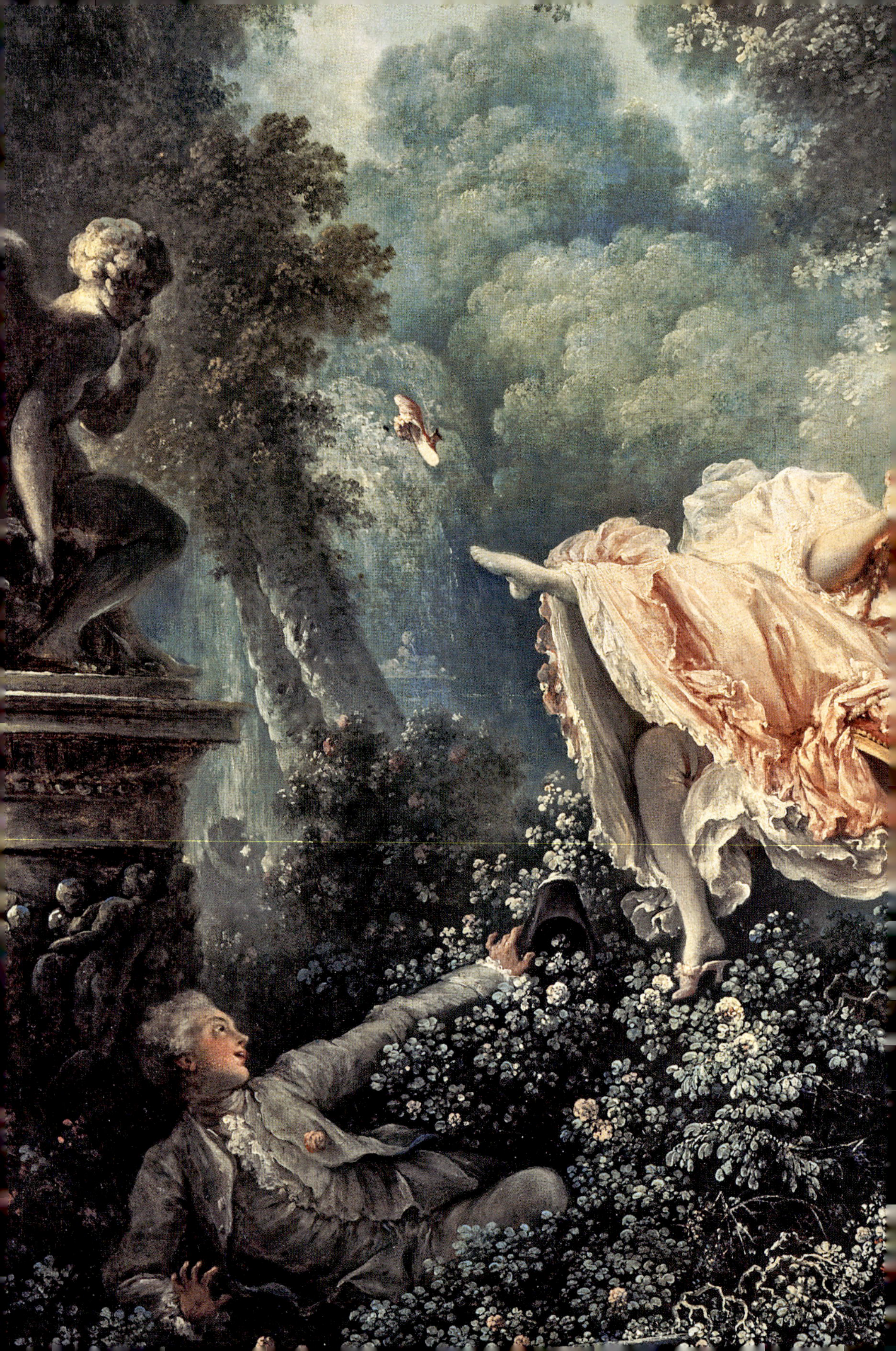

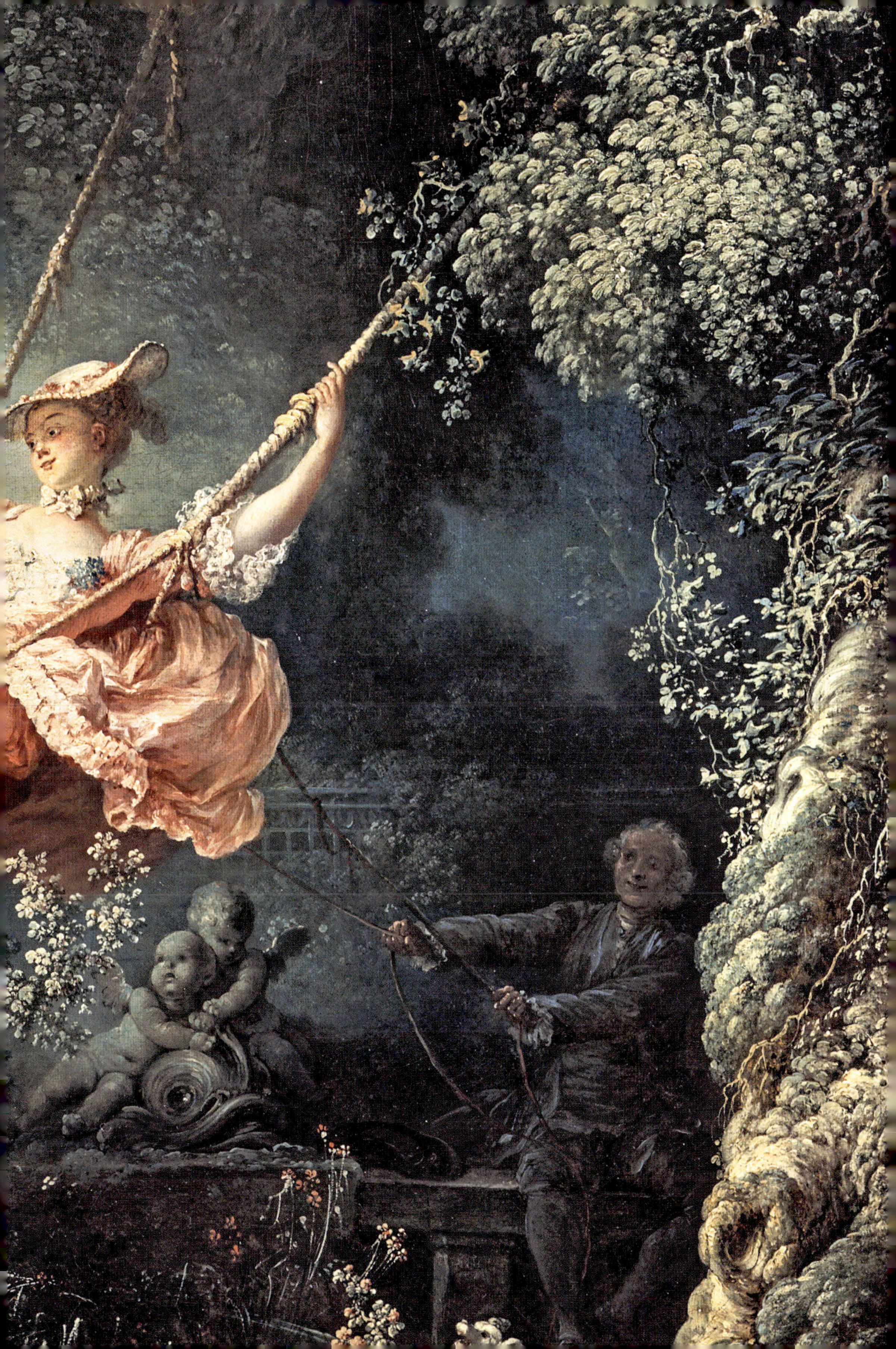

THOMAS GAINSBOROUGH
1727–1788

Perhaps thy love [...] shares thy walk,
With soul to thine attuned. Then Nature all
Wears to the lover's eye a look of love,
And all the tumult of a guilty world,
Tost by ungenerous passions, sinks away.
The tender heart is animated peace [...]

JAMES THOMSON, FROM HIS POEM 'SPRING', PART OF THE SERIES *THE SEASONS* (1730)

On 30 July 1785, two young Londoners, William Hallett (1764–1842) and Elizabeth Stephen (1763/64–1833), wed at the church of St Lawrence in what is now the London Borough of Harrow. Elizabeth was already a wealthy heiress, and the couple were able to afford a double portrait by one of England's most renowned painters, Thomas Gainsborough. It is a work that came to acquire the title *The Morning Walk*.

The painting is a good example of Gainsborough's art at the end of his life. It features bold, 'feathery' brushwork that, when viewed up close, looks a bit like abstract marks. As Gainsborough's contemporary and rival, the painter Joshua Reynolds, said, 'all those odd scratches and marks, which, on a close examination, are so observable in Gainsborough's pictures, and which even to experienced painters appear rather the effect of accident than design – this chaos, this uncouth and shapeless appearance, by a kind of magic, at a certain distance assumes form, and all the parts seem to drop into their proper places'. This style of brushwork gives *The Morning Walk* a hazy, atmospheric quality. Gainsborough's elegant couple stroll with an erect, aristocratic bearing, reflective of an era when wealthy people engaged in formal daily promenades to 'advertise' their union to society. Yet the figures also seem to merge – or almost disappear – into the landscape, somewhat like the elegant pilgrims in Jean-Antoine Watteau's earlier work, *Pilgrimage to the Isle of Cythera* (p. 51). In this way, *The Morning Walk* may suggest a more romantic understanding of the nature of love and the union between husband and wife.

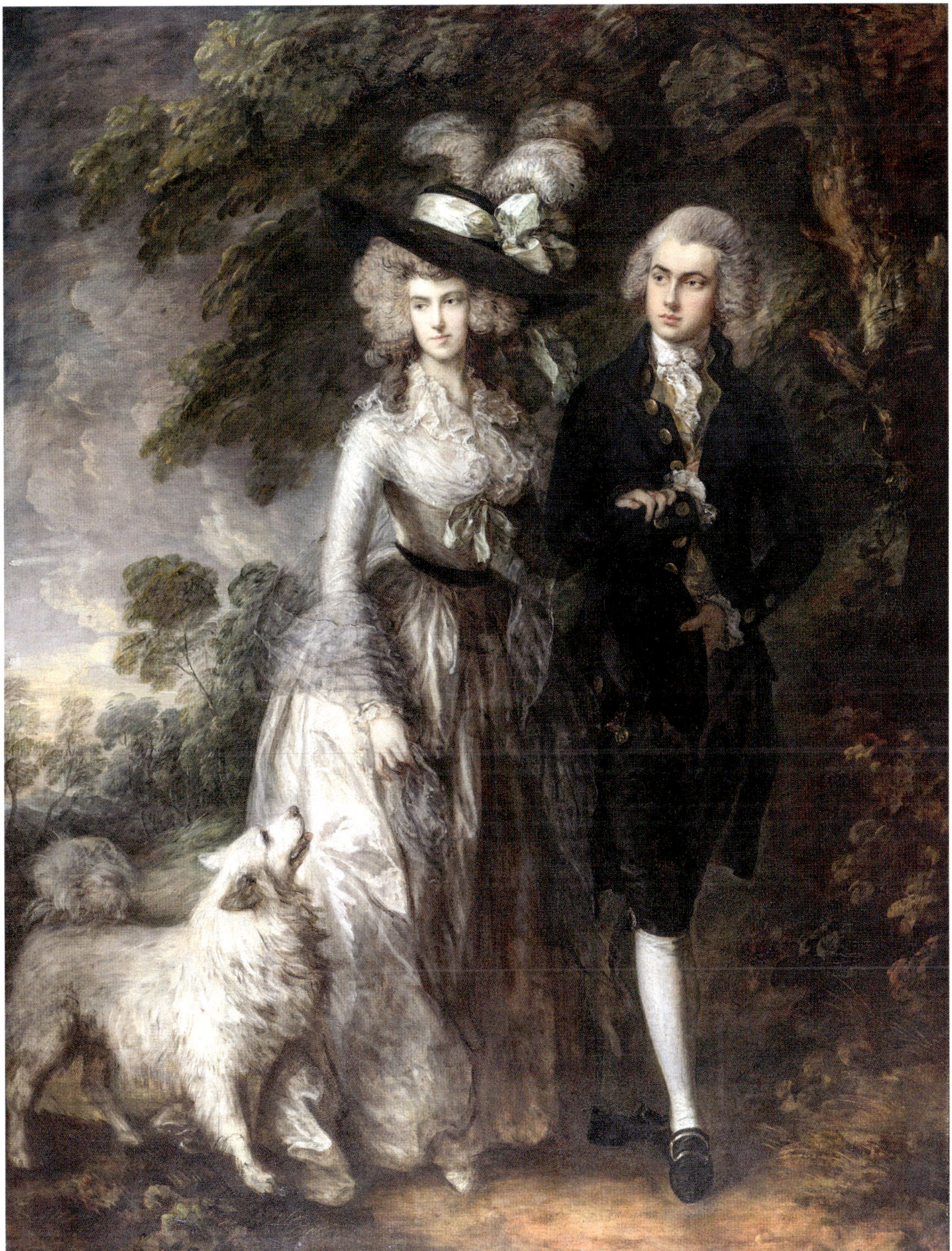

Mr and Mrs William Hallett (The Morning Walk), 1785, oil on canvas, 236.2 × 179.1 cm (93 × 70 ½ in.), The National Gallery, London

KITAGAWA UTAMARO
c. 1754–1806

[...] we could go to see the Japanese prints at the Beaux-Arts.
Seriously, you must not miss that.
You who want to make color prints
you couldn't dream of anything more beautiful.

MARY CASSATT, LETTER TO BERTHA MORISOT (1890)

The ancient temple of Ryūsen-ji, or Meguro Fudō, near Tokyo, is the burial place of a famous romantic couple in Japanese folklore: Shirai Gonpachi and Komurasaki. According to the tale, Shirai Gonpachi was a warrior of the Tottori clan who killed a samurai travelling in western Japan called Honjō Sukedayū. Gonpachi then fled to Edo (present-day Tokyo), where he was caught and sentenced to death in 1679. When his lover, Komurasaki, discovered he had been executed, she travelled to his grave, where she committed suicide. The tragic story of lost love, somewhat reminiscent of Shakespeare's *Romeo and Juliet*, became a popular subject for puppet plays (bunraku) and other forms of traditional Japanese theatre, including kabuki. It also became a subject for Japanese printmakers like Kitagawa Utamaro.

Utamaro worked in a style called ukiyo-e, which typically used woodblock prints to create images of the 'floating world' of geisha, courtesans and actors. These images feature people, often beautiful women, rendered in a stylized, flattened manner, so that they appear to 'float' unnaturally on the two-dimensional page. The work shown here, *The Lovers Miura-ya Komurasaki and Shirai Gonpachi*, from the late Edo period, is characteristic of that style. Faces and clothes are rendered with flowing lines and flat shapes and patterns. The expressions on the two lovers' faces are serene; neither seems to reveal the tragic and violent nature of their love story.

Ukiyo-e art would become extremely popular in Europe during the nineteenth century, especially after 1868, the year Japan ended its long period of isolation from the rest of the world. Japanese prints like those of Utamaro would be collected by Europeans, and they inspired artists to develop new styles of painting and printmaking in Europe – styles such as Post-Impressionism and Expressionism. Painters including Mary Cassatt (1844–1926) and Paul Gauguin (1848–1903), for example, would create images that incorporate, to a certain extent, Utamaro's flattened forms, thus rendering their own 'floating' images of love on canvas and paper.

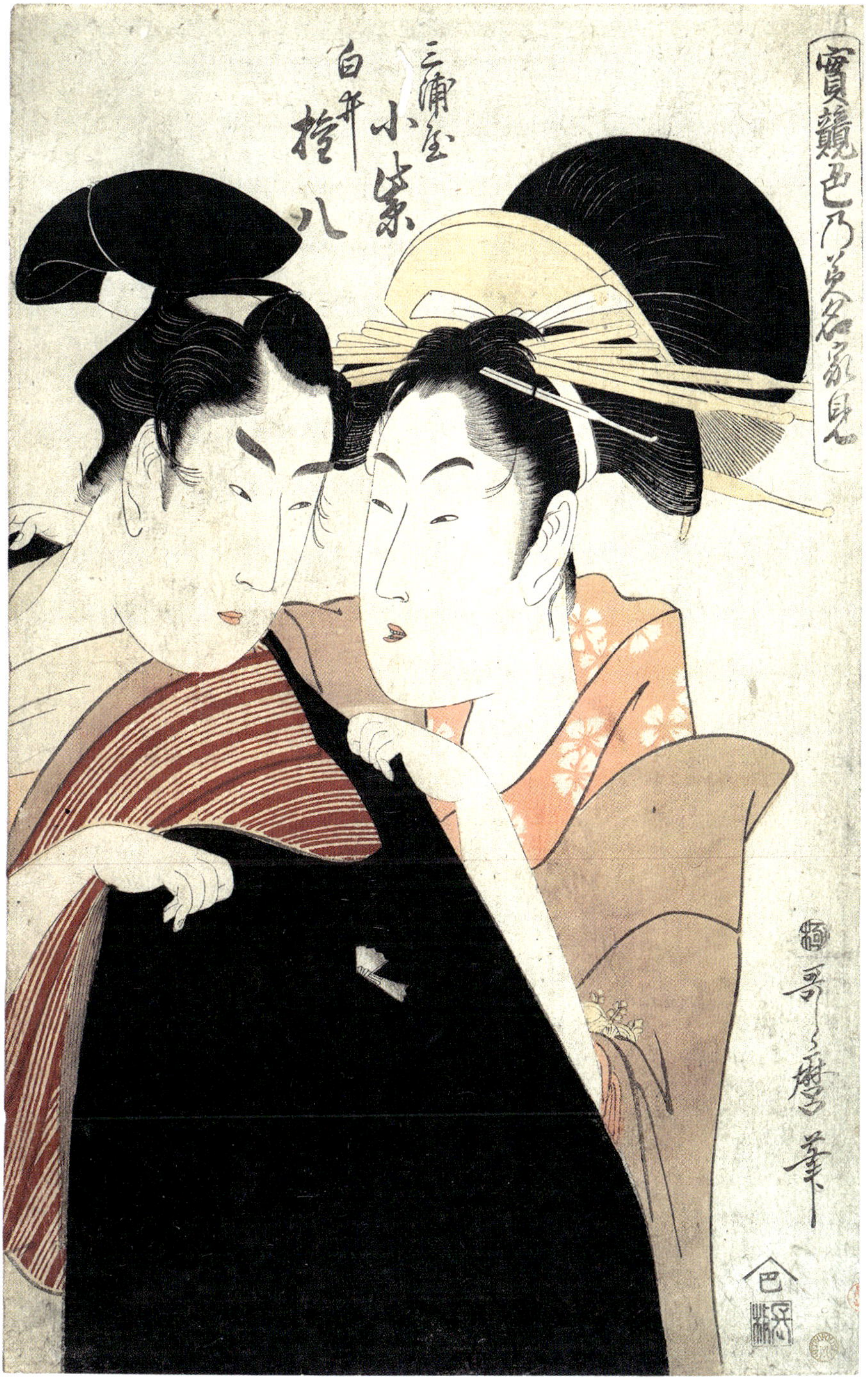

The Lovers Miura-ya Komurasaki and Shirai Gonpachi, c. 1797, woodblock print; ink and colour on paper, 38.1 × 24.1 cm (15 × 9 ½ in.), The Metropolitan Museum of Art, New York

CASPAR DAVID FRIEDRICH
1774–1840

[…] and I can safely say, that the happiest part of my life has been spent on board a ship. While we were together, you know, there was nothing to be feared.

JANE AUSTEN, *PERSUASION* (1817), CHAPTER 8, WHERE MRS CROFT TELLS OF HER LIFE AT SEA WITH ADMIRAL CROFT

German painter Caspar David Friedrich personified the Romantic era of painting like no other. His landscapes are more than detailed reproductions of nature. They seem to embody Friedrich's own moods – longing, alienation and anguish. In 1818, the sensitive artist, who had remained a bachelor into his mid-forties, married Caroline Bommer, a young woman from Dresden. Caroline's brother owned a shop in the city that sold art supplies, and Friedrich may have met his future wife through him. The marriage had a significant impact on Friedrich's art, as he began including Caroline and other female figures more often in his paintings.

In *On the Sailing Boat*, the couple (possibly Friedrich and Caroline themselves) are seen travelling on a fanciful journey at sea. With the wind in their sails, they glide effortlessly towards a hazy town of churches and cathedral spires in the distance. Friedrich's composition places the open, foreshortened hull of the ship, with its tree-like mast, in the foreground – seemingly inviting the viewer to step into the boat and join the voyage. Yet there remains a distance, both visual and emotional, between us and the young couple. Most art historians, in fact, see *On the Sailing Boat* as a metaphor of the 'journey' one embarks upon in marriage.

Friedrich's nautical painting also reminds viewers of the naval traditions in England and other countries at that time, when wives of commanding officers occasionally travelled with their husbands aboard ship. Russian Tsar Nicholas I (1796–1855), who had what was then the second-largest naval fleet in the world, likely purchased the freshly painted *On the Sailing Boat* as early as 1820. It remains today in the collection of the State Hermitage Museum in Saint Petersburg.

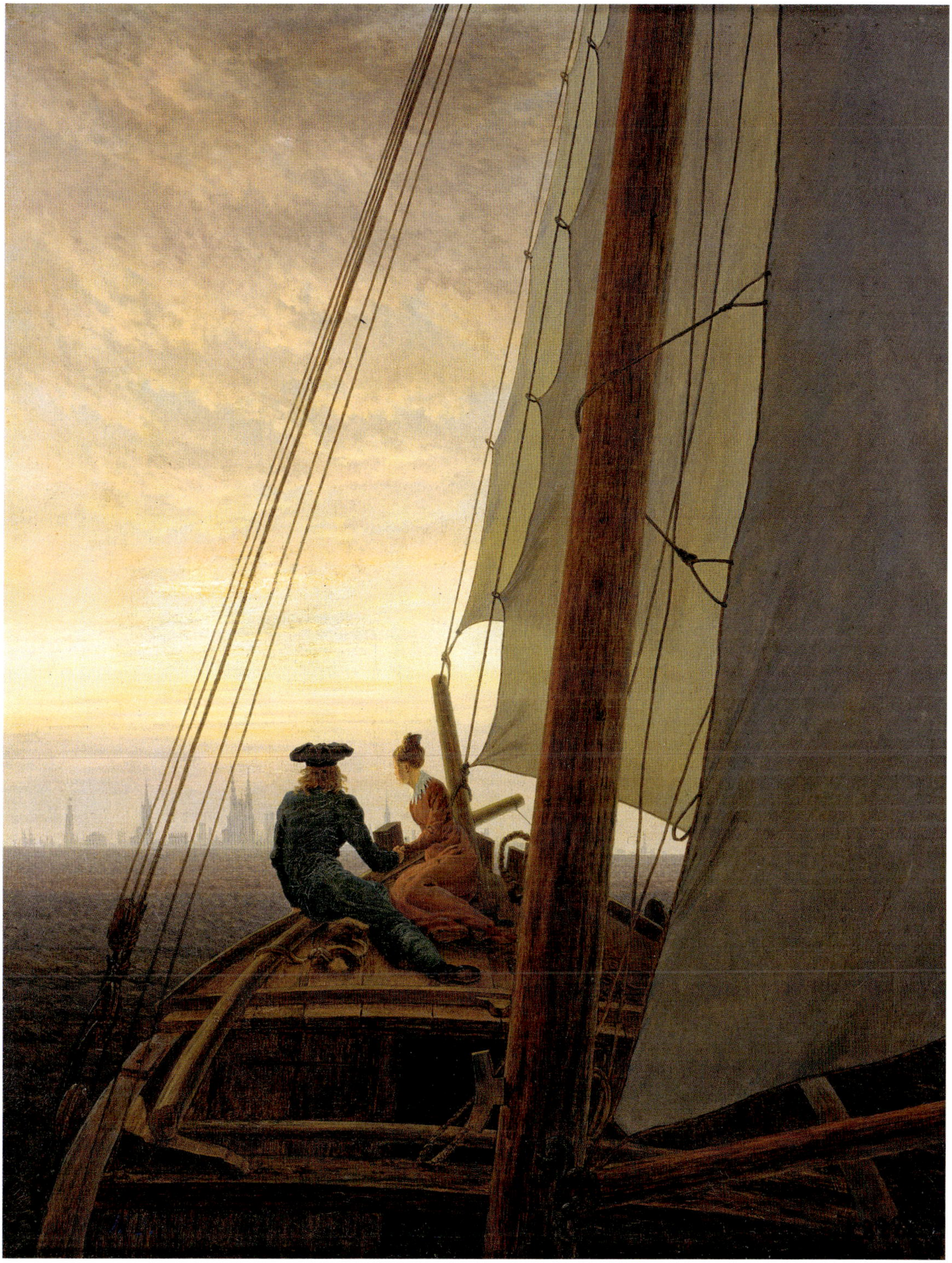

On the Sailing Boat, 1818–1820, oil on canvas,
71 × 56 cm (28 × 22 in.), The State Hermitage Museum, Saint Petersburg

FRANCESCO HAYEZ
1791–1882

Hayez [...] departed from the servile in order to offer a historic and civic ideal that results from his choosing, gleaned from the study of centuries and nations.

DEFENDENTE SACCHI ON BEAUTY AND UGLINESS IN 'A PROVINCIAL IN MILAN: VISITING HAYEZ'S STUDIO' (1830)

The nineteenth century was an age of revolt – a time when love and art were often bound up with politics. Revolutions in the United States and France at the end of the 1700s inspired other places, including Italy, to seek their own independence and nationhood. Throughout most of their long history, Italians had never enjoyed a unified nation. During the Renaissance, large parts of the Italian peninsula were dominated by individual city-states, duchies and princely territories. Eventually, much of Italy came under the control of more powerful European empires, such as the Austrian Habsburg monarchy. But in 1848, Milan and other Italian cities began to rise up and rebel against the Austrians. These uprisings formed part of the Risorgimento, the liberation movement that led to the creation of the Kingdom of Italy and, in 1870, the final unification of the independent nation.

During these years of struggle, Italian artists were among the leading proponents of independence. Francesco Hayez, a Venetian-born painter, settled in Milan in 1822 and began producing images filled with subtle political meaning. In his most famous work, *The Kiss*, we see a pair of lovers in historicized costume embracing passionately. At one level, the picture captures a moment of intense romantic love in a medieval setting – a type of image popular among nineteenth-century artists. But as many historians have noted, the image may also pay homage to a new political era for Italy. The work's dominant colours (the blue and white of the woman's dress and the red of the man's hose) evoke the national colours of France, a nation born out of revolution and one that was currently allied with Italian patriots against the Austrians. Hayez also shows his male figure's left leg set on the stairs at the right, a detail suggesting his kiss may be a farewell gesture before ascending upwards into battle. It is an image that uses romance to pay homage to history, and to inspire a new chapter in that history. Fittingly, *The Kiss* was first exhibited in Milan on 9 September 1859, only three months after that city finally liberated itself from Austrian rule in the Battle of Magenta.

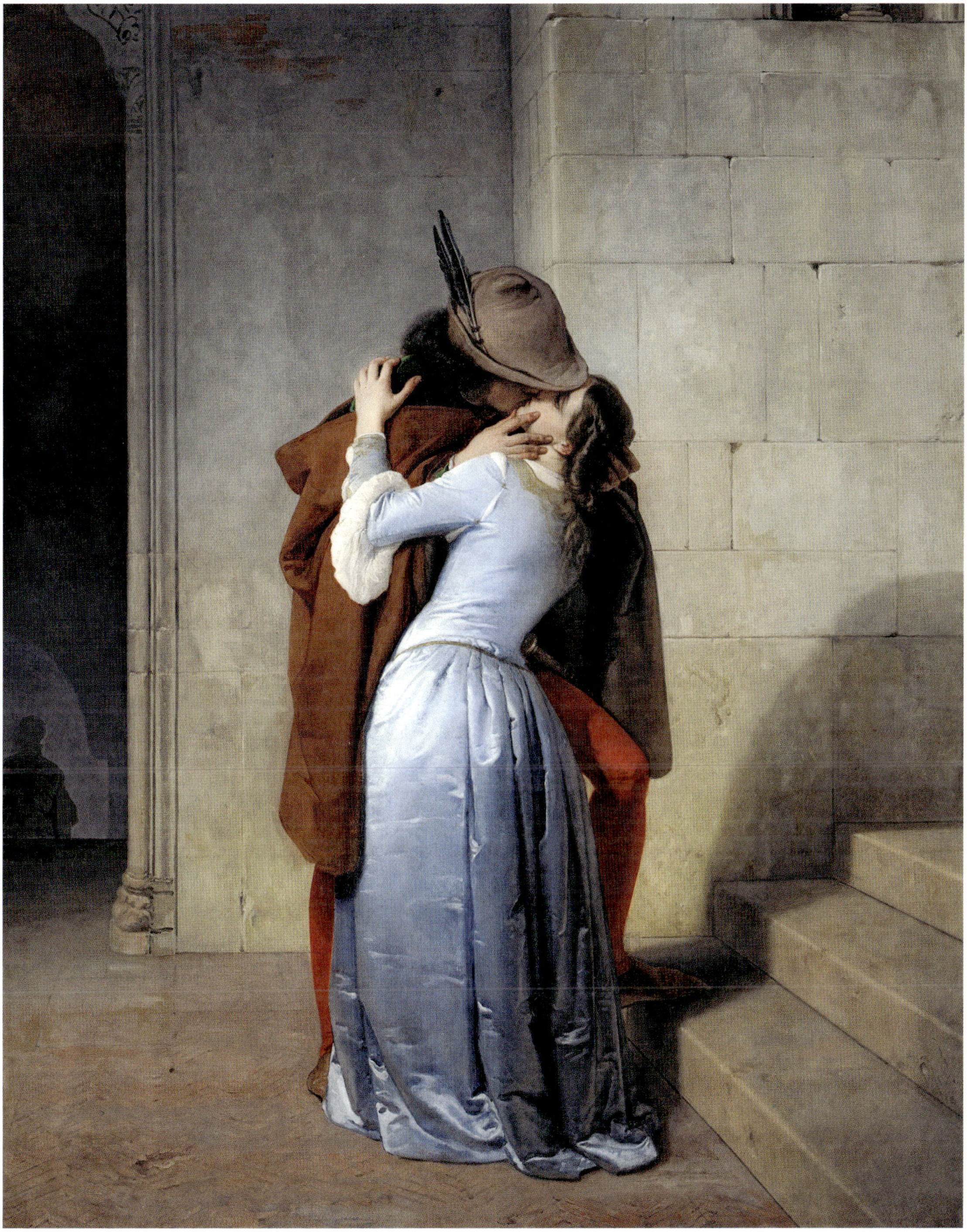

The Kiss, 1859, oil on canvas,
112 × 88 cm (44 ⅛ × 34 ⅝ in.), Pinacoteca di Brera, Milan

ÉDOUARD MANET
1832–1883

The young man and woman are superb. [...]
People eating lunch in real light, in the open air [...]
life shown as it is, without exaggeration.

JORIS-KARL HUYSMANS,
FROM A CRITIQUE OF *CHEZ LE PÈRE LATHUILLE*
AT THE PARIS SALON, *LA RÉFORME* (1880)

Le Père Lathuille was an old-fashioned Parisian restaurant and cabaret near the historic tollhouse at Place de Clichy. It also stood near the Café Guerbois, a well-known hotspot for young artists and other bohemians. The painter Édouard Manet, who spent time at the Guerbois, had become a guiding light for the burgeoning Impressionist movement. Manet helped bring prominence to the Salon des Refusés (Exhibition of Rejects) in 1863, the first ever exhibition of 'outsider' artists. Later salons would highlight the work of early Impressionists like Pierre-Auguste Renoir (1841–1919) and Claude Monet (1840–1926), and by the late 1870s, Manet's own style had adopted many of the Impressionists' techniques.

So in 1879, Manet decided to paint a romantic outdoor scene at Le Père Lathuille. He hired Louis Gauthier-Lathuille, son of the restaurant's owner, as the model for his male figure. The scene was to depict a cavalry officer in uniform with his girlfriend, a common image in the nineteenth century. But in the process of making the picture, Manet changed his mind. According to Gauthier-Lathuille, 'Manet was fidgety. "Take off your jacket and put on mine", he said to me at last, handing me his own jacket of tussore silk. [...] and thus it was decided that I should pose in civilian clothes'. This change in costume helped inspire Manet to create an iconic example of Impressionist art. In *Chez le Père Lathuille* (which roughly means 'At Le Père Lathuille'), we see a casual romantic moment captured in time. The couple are engaged in conversation, the man turned somewhat amorously towards the woman with his hand on the back of her chair; the woman a bit more reticent and erect in posture. Manet's entire scene is bathed in natural light and bright colours. While earlier paintings of love often relied on historical imagery and elevated emotions (see Hayez's *The Kiss*, p. 65), Impressionist artists captured romance as they saw it in the 'open air' of the modern-day world.

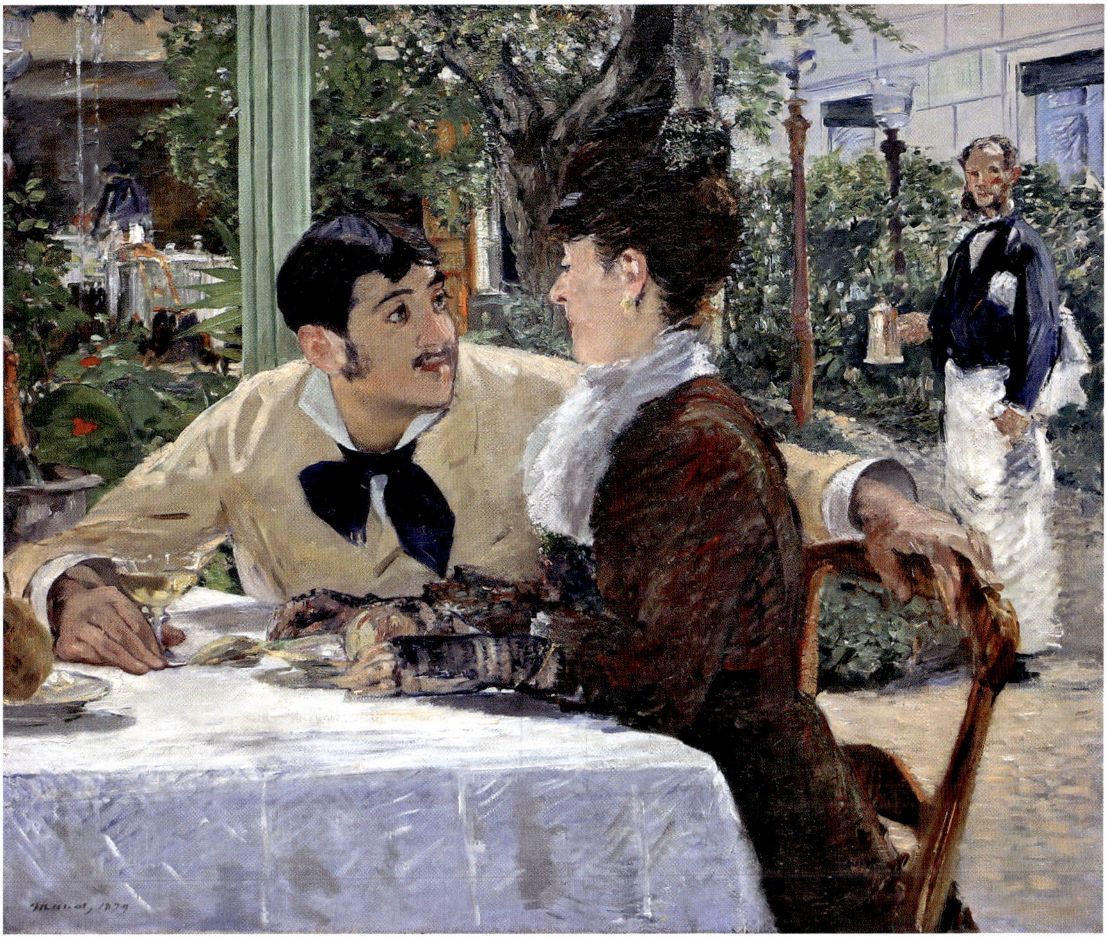

Chez le Père Lathuille, 1879, oil on canvas,
92 × 112 cm (36 × 44 in.), Musée des Beaux-Arts de Tournai

PIERRE-AUGUSTE RENOIR
1841–1919

The world knew how to laugh in those days! Machinery had not absorbed all of life; you had leisure for enjoyment and no one was the worse for it.

PIERRE-AUGUSTE RENOIR
REMEMBERING HIS YOUTH, IN CONVERSATION WITH ART DEALER AMBROISE VOLLARD AND PUBLISHED POSTHUMOUSLY (1919)

Like Manet's *Chez le Père Lathuille* (p. 67), *Dance at Bougival* captures an exquisite, impressionistic moment of love and romance. Painted by Pierre-Auguste Renoir just a few years after Manet's painting, the image shows two lovers in an intimate dance. They are likely enjoying a holiday at the French town of Bougival, only a short train ride outside of Paris. The suburban parish had become a lively hotspot for artists and holidaymakers, with romantic cafés along the Seine River.

The dancing couple, who may be modelled on two of Renoir's friends, are shown in the midst of motion. The woman's dress twirls as she turns with her partner, and her expression – both coy and amorous – reflects the overall mood. They appear almost lost in a mist, as the trees and other customers enjoying drinks seem far removed from the main pair. Renoir achieves this effect by rendering the background in hazy brushwork. What is more, his pastel palette captures the soft light of a lazy afternoon in summer. It is an enchanting scene of two people who have abandoned thoughts of anyone or anything else but themselves.

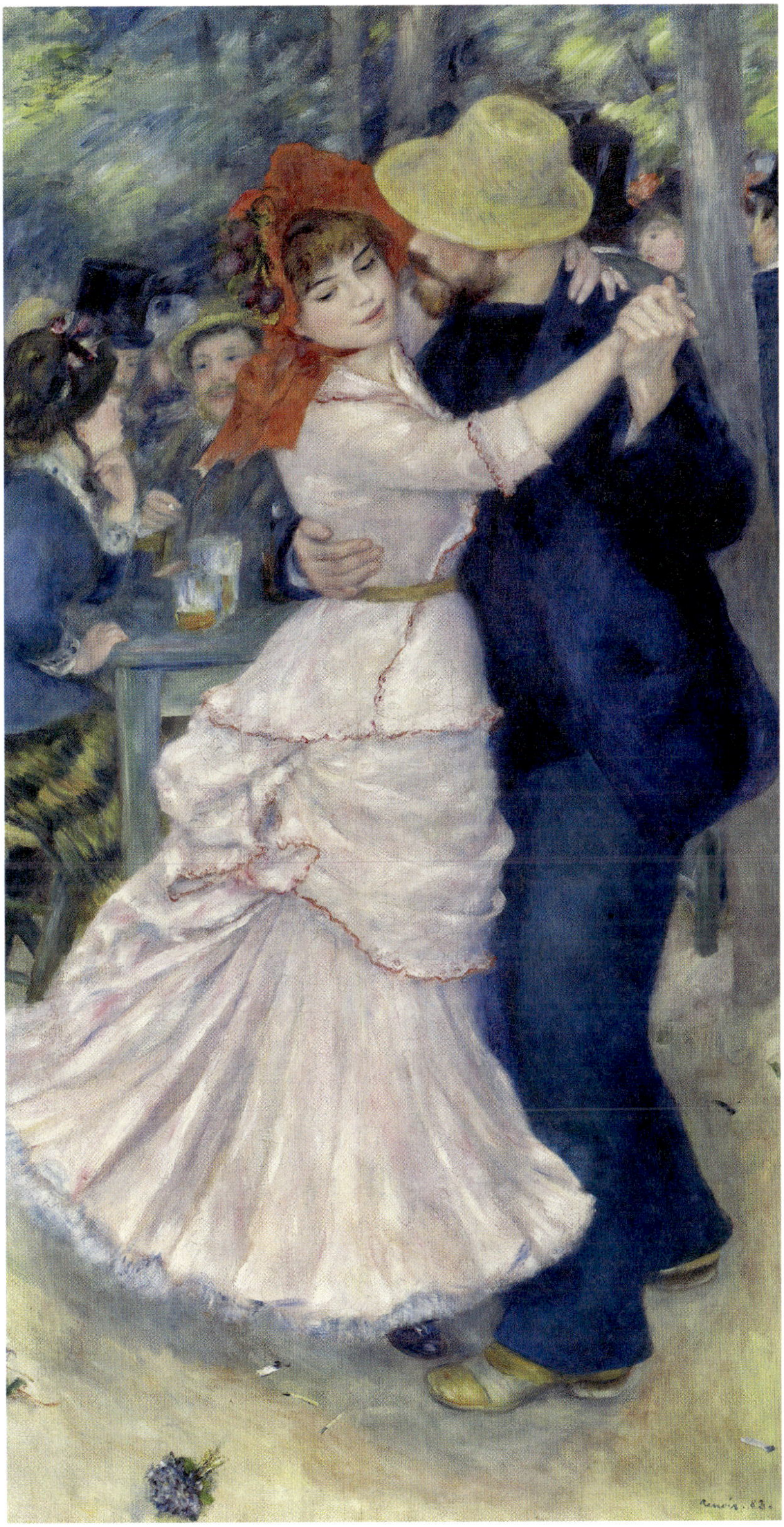

Dance at Bougival, 1883, oil on canvas,
181.9 × 98.1 cm (71 ⅝ × 38 ⅝ in.), Museum of Fine Arts, Boston

AUGUSTE RODIN
1840–1917

The main thing is to be moved, to love, to hope, to tremble, to live.

AUGUSTE RODIN'S 'TESTAMENT' (1911), DICTATED TO PAUL GSELL FOR PUBLICATION AFTER HIS DEATH

In 1880, French sculptor Auguste Rodin was commissioned to design a monumental bronze gateway for a proposed decorative arts museum in Paris. The gate would feature images from *The Divine Comedy*, a long fourteenth-century narrative poem by Dante Alighieri (c. 1265–1321) that describes, in part, a journey through hell. Rodin worked on *The Gates of Hell* for the rest of his life, and he would create several works of sculpture that were intended for the mammoth portal but never made it into the final artwork. One of these sculptures, *Eternal Springtime*, features a man and woman caught in a tender, passionate embrace.

Though it is unclear why *Eternal Springtime* never became part of *The Gates of Hell*, Rodin may have found it too romantic to include in a work representing eternal damnation. Indeed, scholars note that the piece was originally inspired by a 'romantic' concert – a piano duo performance of Beethoven's Second Symphony played by a male and female musician. *Eternal Springtime* does have a musical quality to it. Both figures are caught in the midst of expressive movement. The man appears to be carrying his lover off the ground, while the woman's torso sweeps backwards – her right arm reaching over her head to touch the man's hair. The work's dramatic sense of motion hearkens back to earlier images of passion, such as Bronzino's *An Allegory with Venus and Cupid* (p. 39). Rodin was also inspired by works of ancient Greek art and mythology, which can be seen in the small, vestigial Cupid-like wings he added to the male figure. This classical detail may refer to the eternal nature of love itself. For Rodin, it appears, love was both timeless and something that could be caught in the moment.

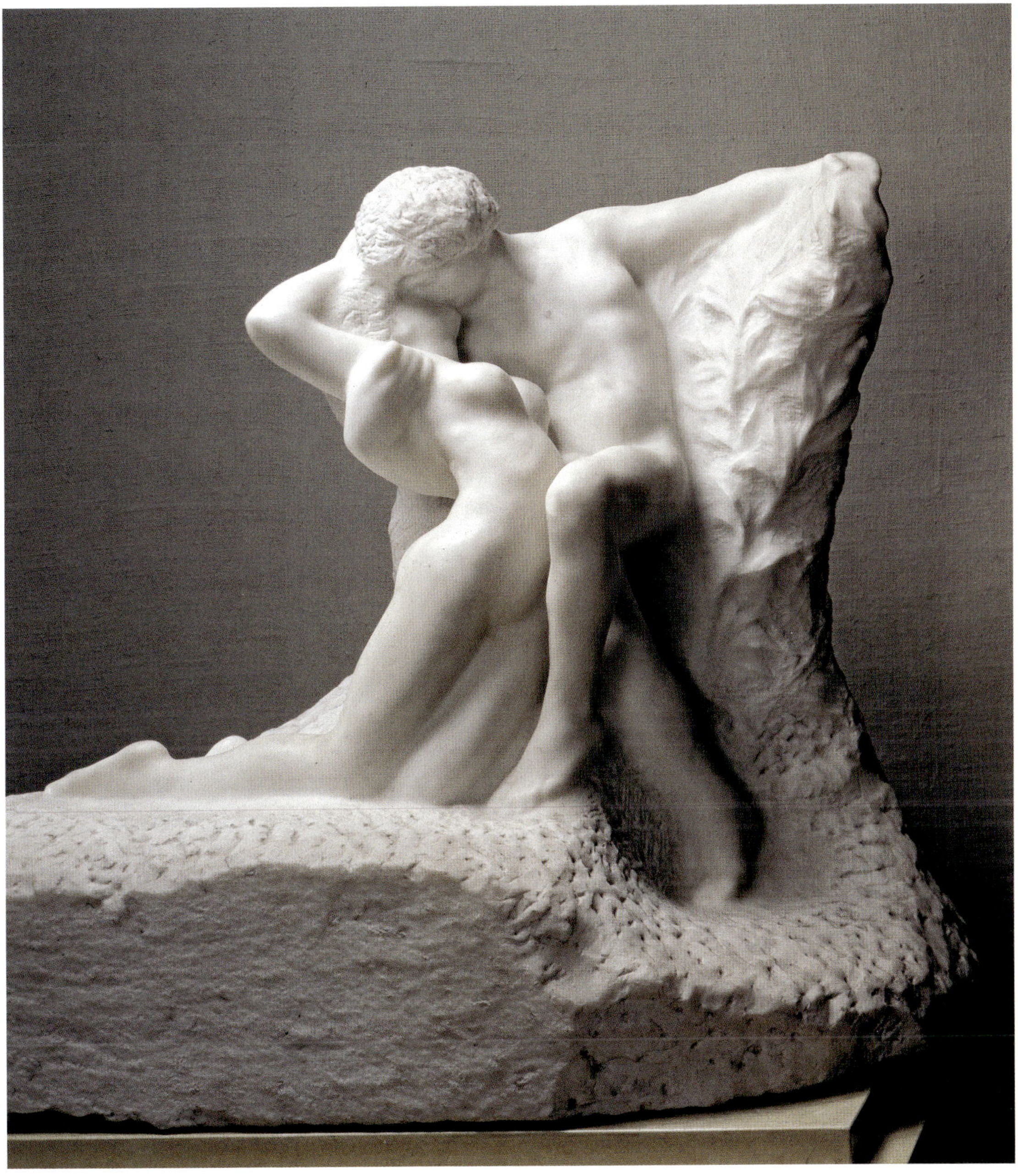

Eternal Springtime, 1884, marble,
40 × 52 × 32.5 cm (15 ¾ × 20 ½ × 12 ¾ in.), Museo Soumaya, Mexico City

FREDERIC LEIGHTON
1830–1896

Then bending gently back her head,
With that sweet mouth, so rosy red,
Upon his eyes she dropped a kiss,
Intoxicating him with bliss.

CATULLUS, POEM 45 (MID-1ST CENTURY BC), IN THEODORE MARTIN'S RHYMING TRANSLATION, AS PRINTED IN THE CATALOGUE OF THE ONE HUNDREDTH EXHIBITION OF THE ROYAL ACADEMY OF ARTS, LONDON (1868)

The art world of Victorian England was a mix of staid realism and the avant-garde. Traditional painters who studied at the Royal Academy produced sombre, highly naturalistic images that were influenced by earlier British masters like Joshua Reynolds or Thomas Gainsborough (p. 59). Other artists, however, were beginning to rebel against these older traditions. The Pre-Raphaelites, for example, experimented with vivid colours and with human figures rendered in the manner of Early Renaissance artists like Botticelli (p. 25).

Frederic Leighton was an artist who, in some ways, straddled the traditional and modern worlds. Born into a wealthy family, he became a long-time member and President of the Royal Academy. But he was also a supporter of many Pre-Raphaelite artists, including Edward Burne-Jones (1833–1898) and Dante Gabriel Rossetti (1828–1882). His own style, in fact, displayed some of the livelier qualities of Pre-Raphaelite art.

Acme and Septimus is a good example of Leighton's style. It was based on a love poem by the Roman poet Catullus (c. 84–c. 54 BC), where the fictional lovers Acme and Septimus are struck (or 'sneezed' on) by Amor, the spirit of love, to solidify their pledge of loyalty to each other. Leighton was particularly inspired by the passage describing Acme as 'bending gently back her head', a passage that Leighton renders here with soft elegance. *Acme and Septimus* also incorporates interesting shapes. The work as a whole is done on a round canvas (or tondo), a format favoured by Botticelli, while the two lovers are grouped in a triangular form. This latter compositional style has its origins in the Renaissance, especially in paintings by Raphael. But despite its traditional qualities, *Acme and Septimus* also has a natural, intimate air. We could almost see its 'mythological' couple as modern-day lovers enjoying an afternoon out, but who happen to be clothed in ancient dress.

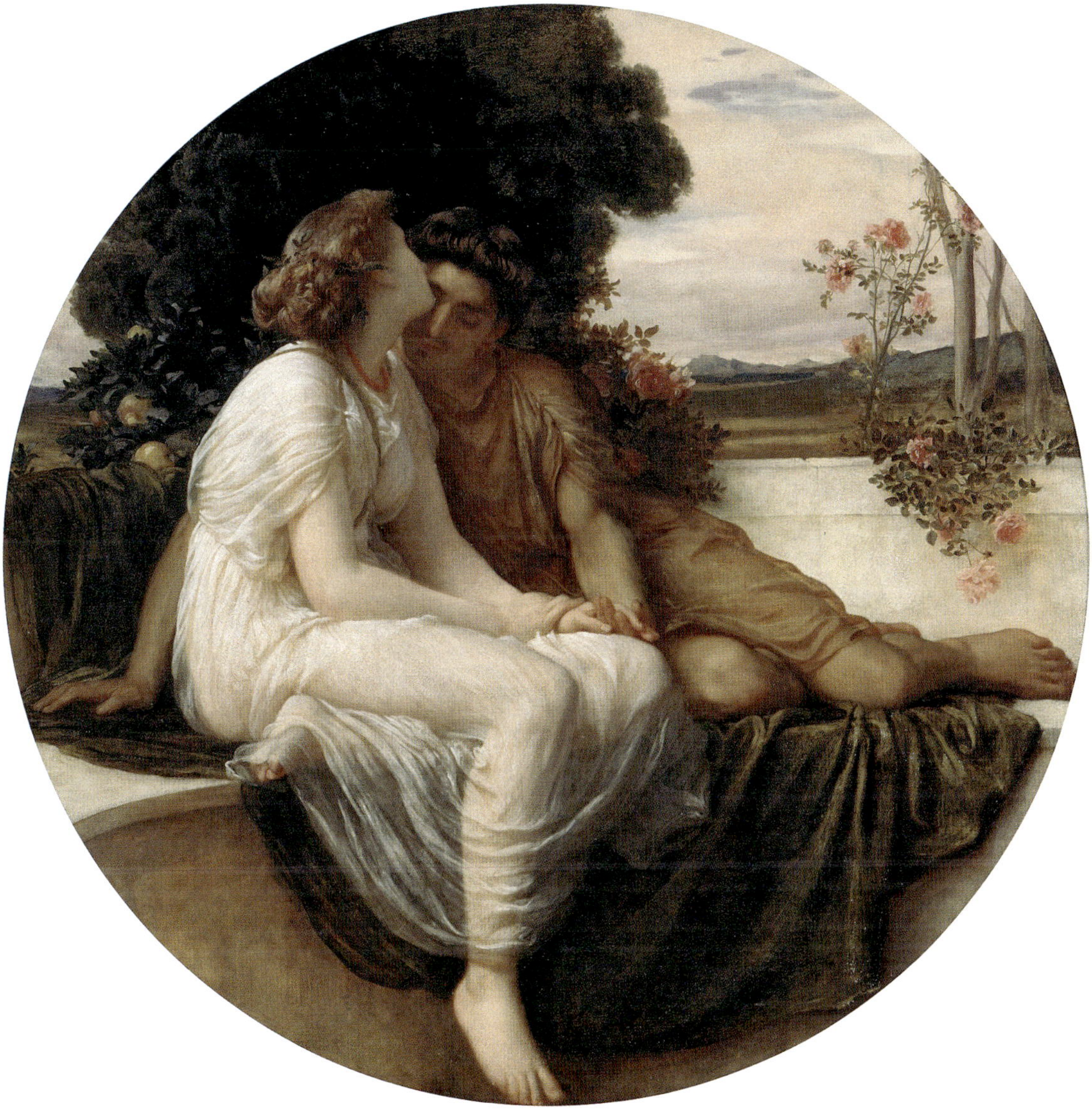

Acme and Septimus, 1868, oil on canvas, diameter 99 cm (39 in.),
Ashmolean Museum, Oxford

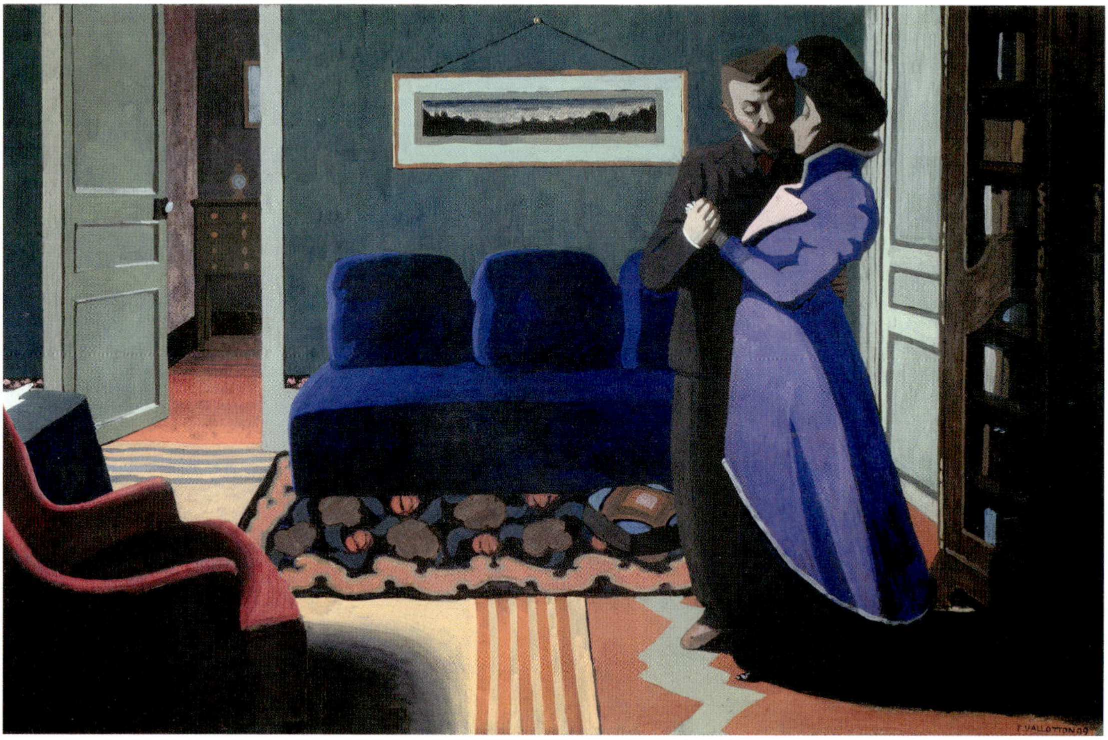

The Visit, 1899, gouache on board,
55 × 87 cm (21 ⅝ × 34 ¼ in.), Kunsthaus Zürich

FÉLIX VALLOTTON
1865–1925

*Ten times a man and a woman meet in all of
the attitudes in which the mishaps,
the stages of sentimental life are fixed.
They express every imaginable aspect, the naïve and the ridiculous,
the hypocrisy and the lies, the cruelty
and the taste for death that is in all of our conception of love.*

THADÉE NATANSON, 'ON M. FÉLIX VALLOTTON',
ARTICLE IN *LA REVUE BLANCHE* (1899)

The nineteenth century ushered in radical changes in society, from the growing Industrial Revolution to technological innovations like the electric light and the automobile, as well as photography and film. These changes led to a mass migration from farms and small towns to cities, and they produced a feeling of alienation and unease among many artists and writers. Nineteenth-century artists, especially those at the end of the century, expressed such feelings in works that critiqued traditional notions of love and marriage.

One such artist was the Swiss-born painter and printmaker Félix Vallotton. Vallotton's long career is often best remembered for his woodblock prints, which helped re-establish this historical art form in the twentieth century. One early series of prints from the 1890s, called *Intimités* (Intimacies), gained the young artist critical acclaim. These 'intimate' interior scenes offered striking critiques of mainstream domestic life. Rendered in harsh black-and-white contrasts with deep shading, the works feel emotionally barren and somewhat toxic. Married couples are shown going through the motions of married life, but without any real passion or feelings of conjugal love.

Vallotton followed up *Intimités* with a group of paintings that covered the same themes. One of the best of these, *The Visit*, shows a husband and wife entering a domestic space devoid of all charm. The dull green of the walls, the darkened blue of the couch and the overall atmosphere seem oppressive. The couple hold each other in a position superficially reflective of a dance, but the details of their faces are nearly stripped away, making them look more robotic than human. Vallotton's image captures a stifling world where love and passion are mechanically performed rather than felt.

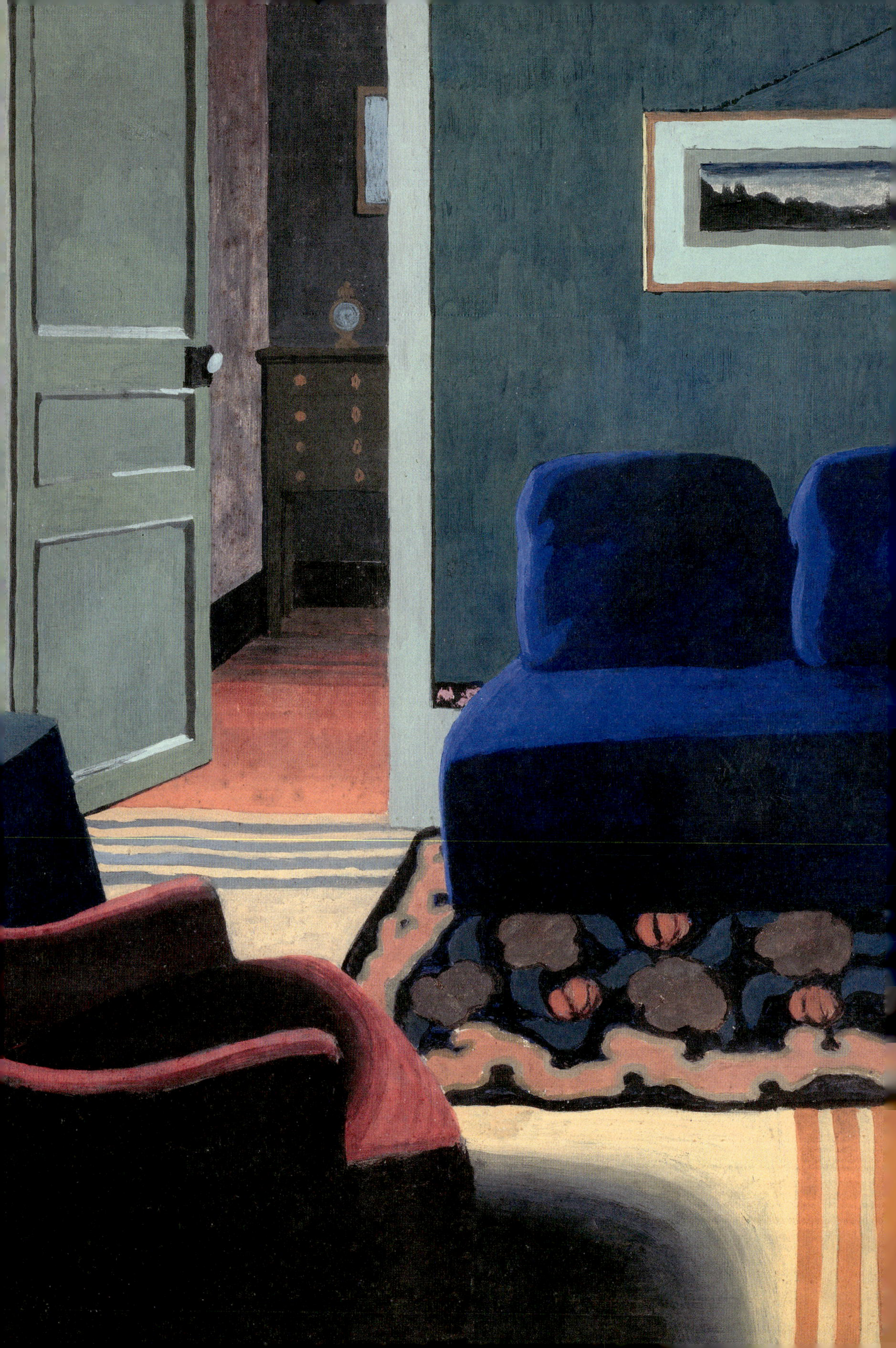

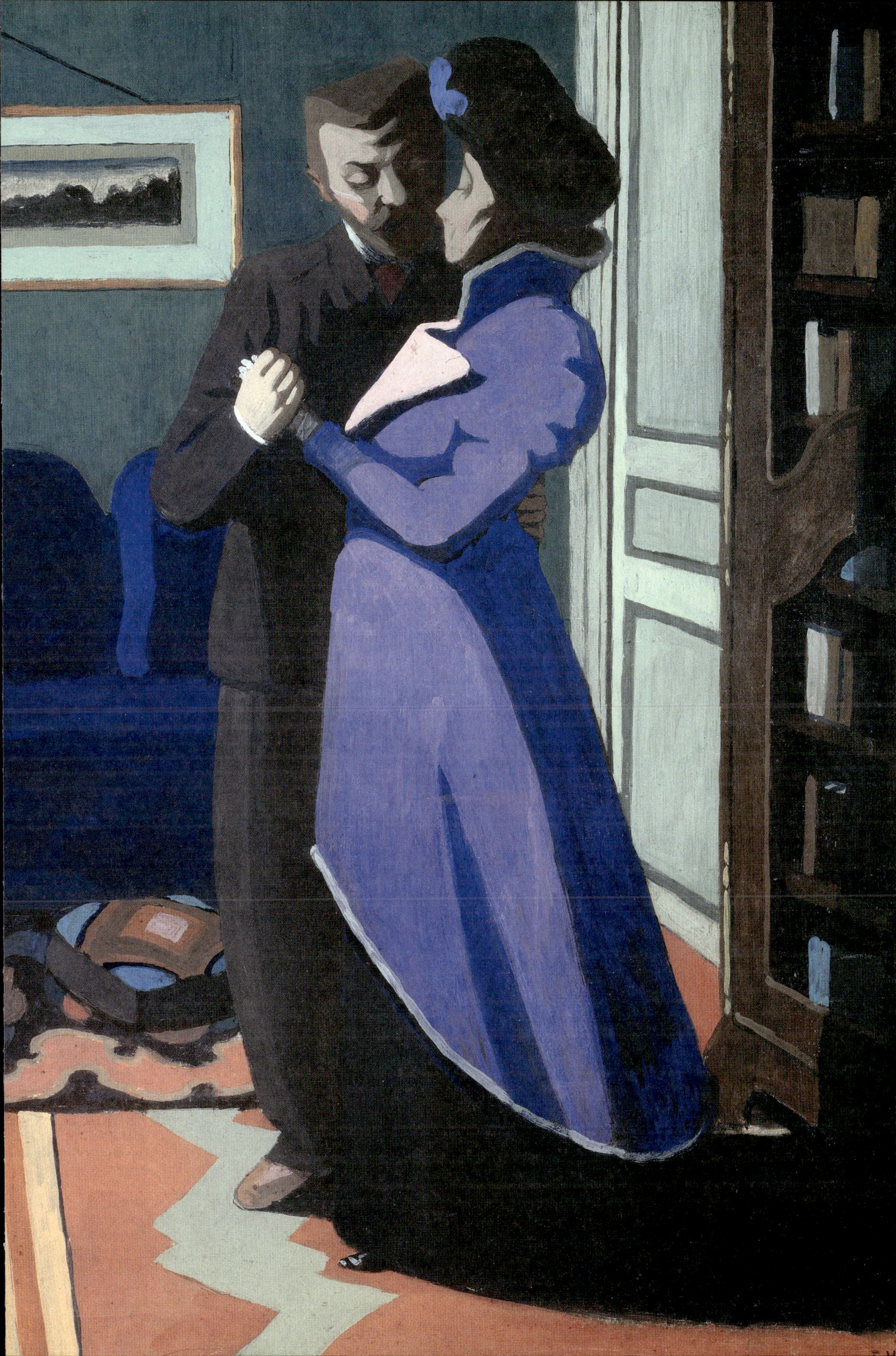

EDVARD MUNCH

1863–1944

*I am dancing with my true love – a memory of her.
A smiling, blonde-haired woman enters who wishes to take the
flower of love – but it won't allow itself to be taken.
And on the other side one can see her dressed in black troubled by
the couple dancing – rejected – as I was rejected from her dance.*

EDVARD MUNCH, DESCRIPTION OF *THE DANCE OF LIFE* FROM HIS DIARIES (c. 1900)

Like the interiors of Félix Vallotton (p. 74), the paintings of Edvard Munch often express the dark side of love. Growing up in Oslo (then Kristiania), Norway, Munch's childhood and adolescence were marked by poverty and death. Born into a family plagued by mental and physical illness, Munch struggled with mental health and addiction throughout his life, battles that may have prevented him from establishing long-term relationships with women. Two of his most prominent affairs were an early tryst with Milly Thaulow (1860–1937, an actress and married woman whom he referred to as 'Mrs Heiberg'), and, later on, Tulla Larsen (1869–1942), one of his models. Both relationships ended in bitter separation.

Munch's personal struggles are often reflected in his art, especially in works like *The Dance of Life*. This painting was one of the last created for Munch's 'Frieze of Life', a series of images – meant to be seen together – that captured in part the psychological undertones of love and abandonment. In *The Dance of Life*, we see a series of individuals and couples dancing at sunset near a coastline. Historians often describe the reflection of the sun's rays on the water as a phallic symbol. In the middle ground, the couples seem free-spirited and youthful, possibly in the early stages of romance. In the foreground, however, the faces begin to look weathered or mask-like, with the rigid central couple (likely a 'portrait' of Munch and Mrs Heiberg) showing stiff, almost mummy-like expressions. In Munch's diary, he described this woman as a 'memory' of his 'true love', but a memory tinged with feelings of rejection. Munch also describes the two blonde-haired women on either side of the dancing couple as different representations of the same person – one of whom wishes to take 'the flower of love', while the other is cast out, dressed in mourning. They are likely different aspects of Tulla Larsen, with whom Munch had just started a relationship. All in all, *The Dance of Life* reveals Munch's understanding of love as temporary and easily lost or ossified over time. The power of the artist's feelings is shown in his intense colours, the often-ghoulish facial expressions and the swirling lines of his dancing bodies.

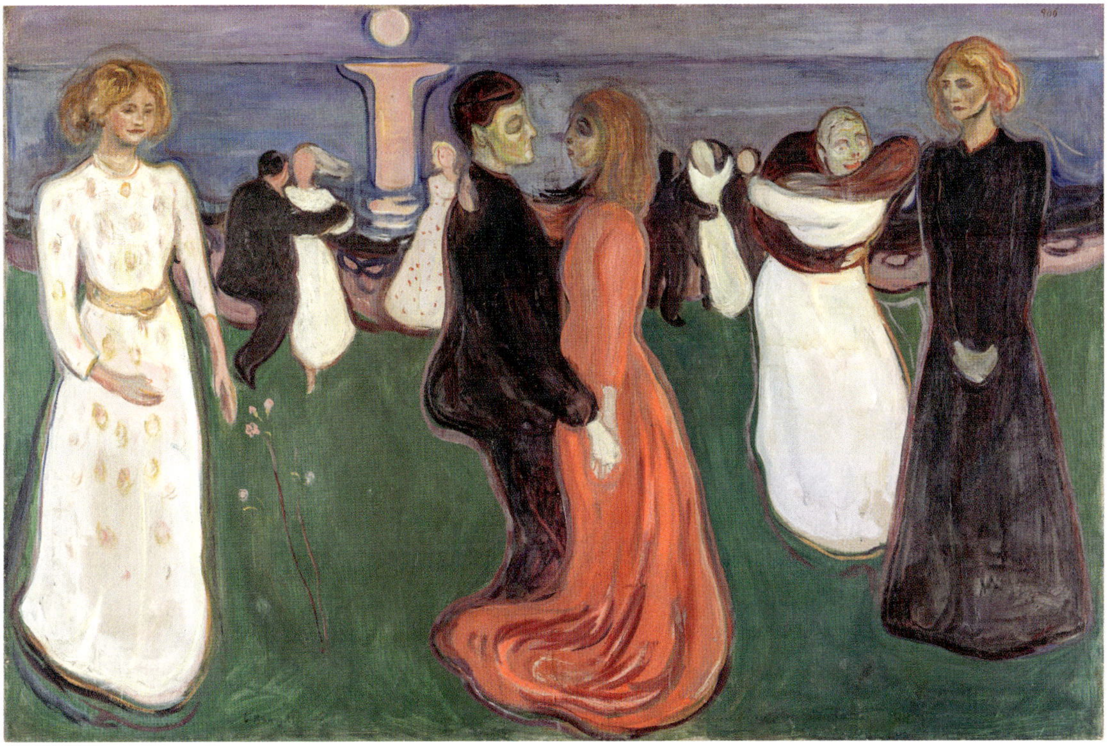

The Dance of Life, 1899–1900, oil on canvas,
125 × 191 cm (49 ¼ × 75 ¼ in.), Nasjonalmuseet, Oslo

CONSTANTIN BRÂNCUȘI
1876–1957

The stone carving of the clasped lovers called The Kiss *is a monument in the lives of two lovers, made immortal.*

JEANNE ROBERT FOSTER,
'NEW SCULPTURES BY CONSTANTIN BRANCUSI',
AN ARTICLE FOR *VANITY FAIR* (1922)

During the early part of his career, Romanian sculptor Constantin Brâncuși spent a brief spell as an assistant in the studio of nineteenth-century master Auguste Rodin. Brâncuși would later admit that 'Without the discoveries of Rodin, my work would have been impossible.' But Brâncuși's work would also depart radically from that of Rodin. Compare Brâncuși's *The Kiss* (the earliest version of which was made in 1905) with Rodin's images of love from the late nineteenth century – works such as *The Kiss* (1882) and *Eternal Springtime* (1884, p. 71). These earlier pieces retain, to an extent, the naturalism of traditional, academic European art. They also present the male/female relationship as a hierarchy, with the man either towering over the woman or appearing to sweep her off the ground. But all 'romantic' traditions are abandoned by Brâncuși. His lovers appear as abstract, rounded forms of the same size and height, with little to distinguish one sex from the other. Their embrace, too, is anything but traditional. It is as if we were witnessing two primitive life forms, such as amoebas or other single-celled organisms, join together.

Though a modern piece, Brâncuși's *Kiss* was inspired by archaic or prehistoric art, which also rendered human figures in stylized, geometric shapes. The work was to have great influence over modern sculpture. It was included in the 1913 Armory Show in New York, the first major exhibition of contemporary Modernist art outside of Europe. Brâncuși even received mention in popular American magazines like *Vanity Fair* in the early decades of the twentieth century. He would continue to explore the theme of love throughout his life, developing many different versions of *The Kiss*. One version, called *The Gate of the Kiss*, was designed as an architectural monument in his home country of Romania.

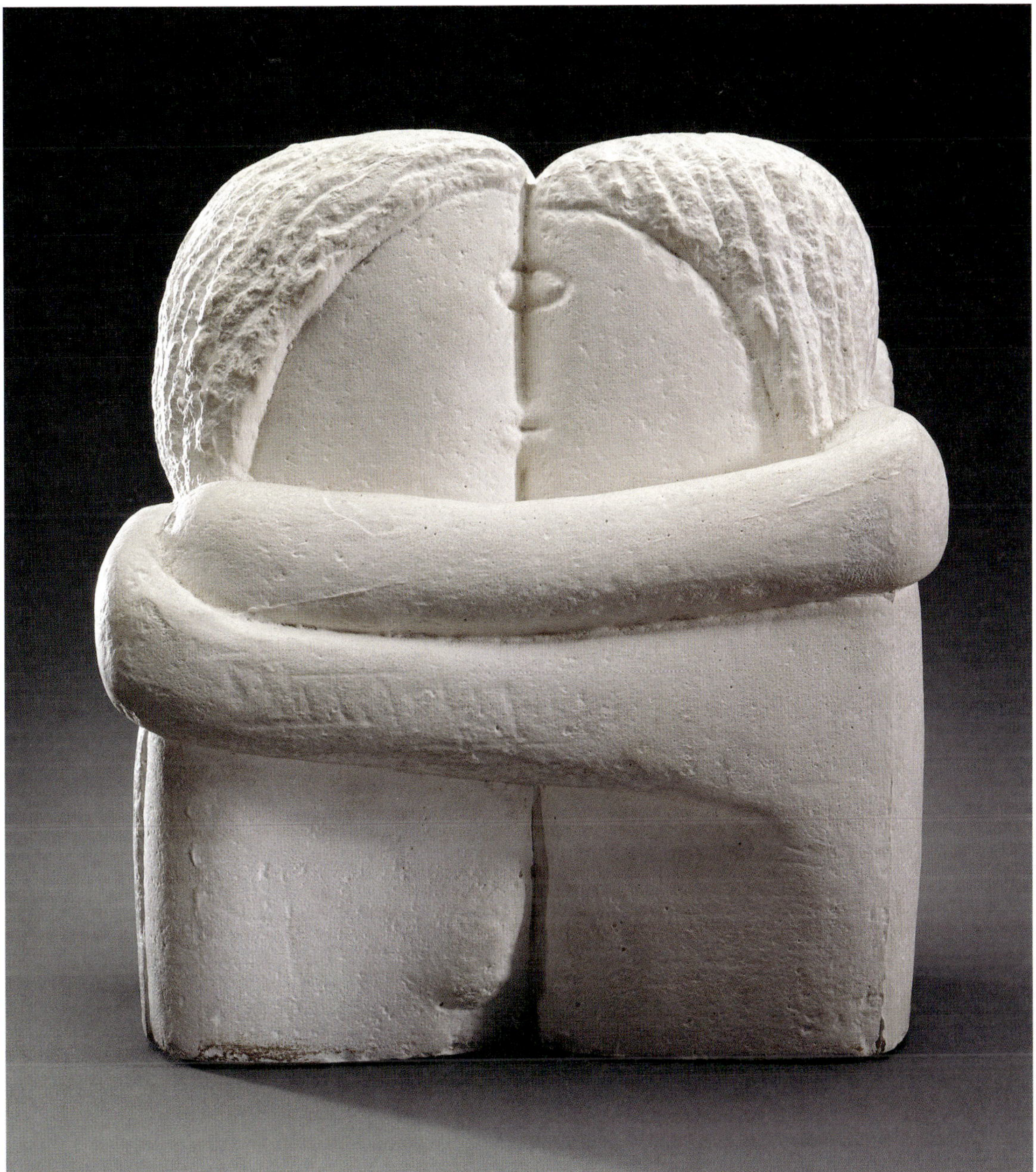

The Kiss, 1907, marlstone,
27.9 × 26 × 21.6 cm (11 × 10 ¼ × 8 ½ in.), Muzeul de Artă din Craiova

HENRI MATISSE

1869–1954

His canvas, which will not be understood,
is called Le Bonheur de vivre.
Creatures in languorous attitudes, with lovely hips, sleep, dream;
one, standing, is stretching, hands crossed behind her head;
others are playing the panpipe;
at right, a slender girl is throwing her arms behind her,
enlacing her lover's head in that cool ring [...]
a sensation of refreshing joy emanates from this canvas.

LOUIS VAUXCELLES, IN A DESCRIPTION OF *LE BONHEUR DE VIVRE* SHOWN AT THE SALON DES INDÉPENDANTS, FOR A REVIEW IN *GIL BLAS* (1906)

With his 1906 article for the literary magazine *Gil Blas*, French art critic Louis Vauxcelles (1870–1943) became one of the few contemporary critics to offer praise for Henri Matisse's revolutionary work *Le Bonheur de vivre* or *The Joy of Life*. The painting was exhibited at the Salon des Indépendants, an unjuried art exhibition that offered a venue for avant-garde artists rejected by the official Salon. These exhibits had featured cutting-edge Parisian work since the days of Édouard Manet. But for many, Matisse's work went too far. Gone was any traditional sense of space, perspective or natural form. Nude revellers appeared to be floating uneasily in a 'landscape' of garishly bright colours. People and trees were reduced to cartoonish outlines, and the overall impression of the work was, for many, one of disquiet – far from the joyous quality of the work's title.

But it was Vauxcelles's opinion that would eventually win the day. With this canvas, Matisse had helped create a new way of understanding art. He had already been a key member of a revolutionary art group called 'les Fauves' (or 'the Wild Beasts'), which used vivid, non-realistic colours and simplified shapes. But *Le Bonheur de vivre*, with its bold, undefined space, would take modern art a step further. Matisse's restless, vivid image makes an emotional impact on the viewer, a reflection of the passionate 'lovers' embracing in the work's right foreground. It is an expression of love in almost primitive form.

The work would also have a strong impact on Pablo Picasso (p. 93), who created his own revolutionary masterpiece, *Les Demoiselles d'Avignon*, the following year. The era of modernism had begun.

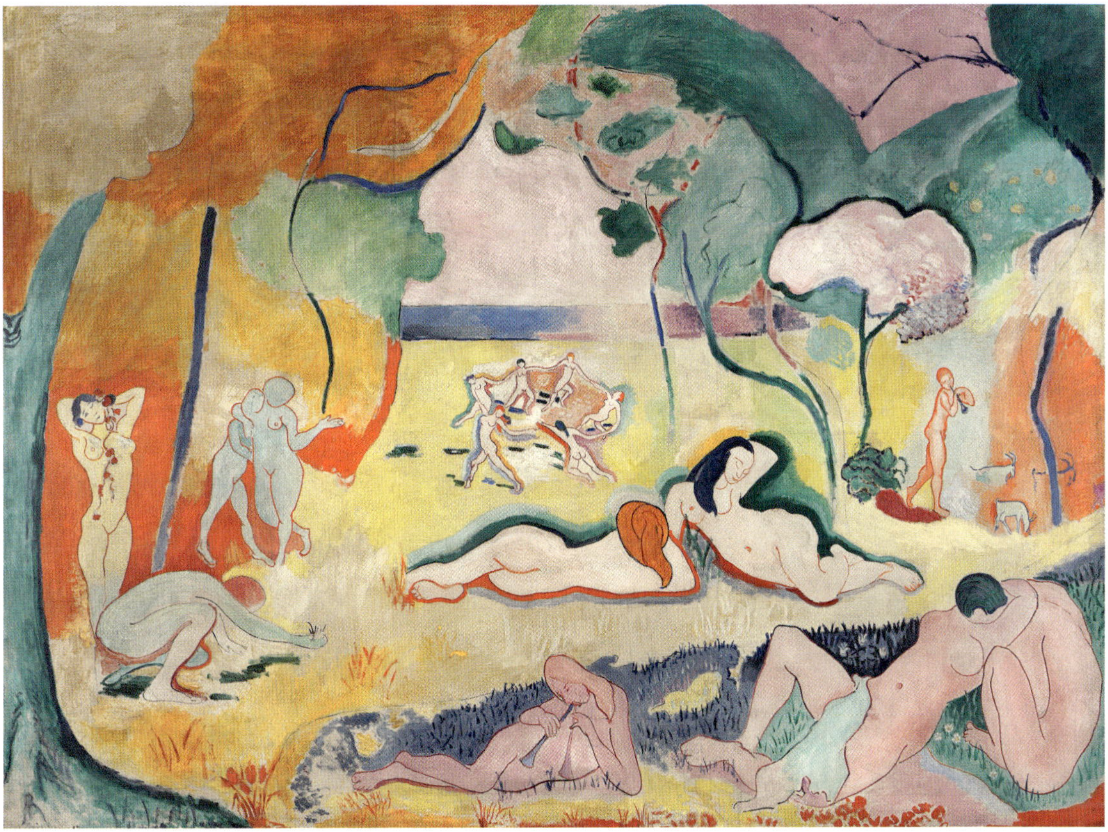

Le Bonheur de vivre (The Joy of Life), 1905/06, oil on canvas,
176.5 × 240.7 cm (69 ½ × 94 ¾ in.), Barnes Foundation, Philadelphia

GUSTAV KLIMT
1862–1918

Gustav Klimt's fateful moment had arrived.
For the gleaming gold mosaics in the churches of Ravenna
made a tremendous, decisive impression on him.
From then on its magnificence,
its frozen splendour was a feature of his sensitive art.

WILHELM DESSAUER, FROM THE REMINISCENCES OF PAINTER MAXIMILIAN LENZ, 'GUSTAV KLIMT'S WINTER JOURNEY TO ITALY' (1933)

In 1903, Austrian painter Maximilian Lenz (1860–1948) accompanied his friend and fellow artist Gustav Klimt on a memorable journey to Italy. While in Ravenna, Klimt explored the city's churches and mausoleums, with their dazzling Byzantine Christian mosaics. Lenz, in a later discussion with painter Wilhelm Dessauer (1882–1943), told of the powerful impression these historic works of art made on Klimt. Their shimmering colours and use of gold, as well as the flattened way Byzantine artists portrayed human figures, would have a profound influence on Klimt's own work – and the work of other Art Nouveau painters.

Klimt's masterpiece, *The Kiss*, reflects much of what he saw at Ravenna. The two embracing lovers are shown in a completely two-dimensional space. This flatness is further emphasized by their clothing, rendered as Byzantine-like patterns of shapes and colours, almost completely obscuring the curves and shapes of their natural bodies. 'Masculine' rectangular forms decorate the man's robe, and rounded, more colourful 'feminine' shapes adorn the woman's dress. Other aspects of the painting, such as the flowery ground beneath their feet, and the sharply asymmetrical composition, may be inspired by another historically 'flattened' art form: the Japanese woodblock print (p. 61).

The Kiss, however, is also a work of its own time. Klimt captures a more modern understanding of sexual passion by the ecstatic look on the woman's face and the somewhat aggressive nature of their embrace. Vienna in 1908 was experimenting with greater sexual freedom; Klimt himself had an open sexual life with many different women. It was also the age of Sigmund Freud, whose writings explored the psychological impact of sexual desire. With *The Kiss*, Klimt offered his own reflection on the eternal nature of love, as well as the changing mores around how love was expressed.

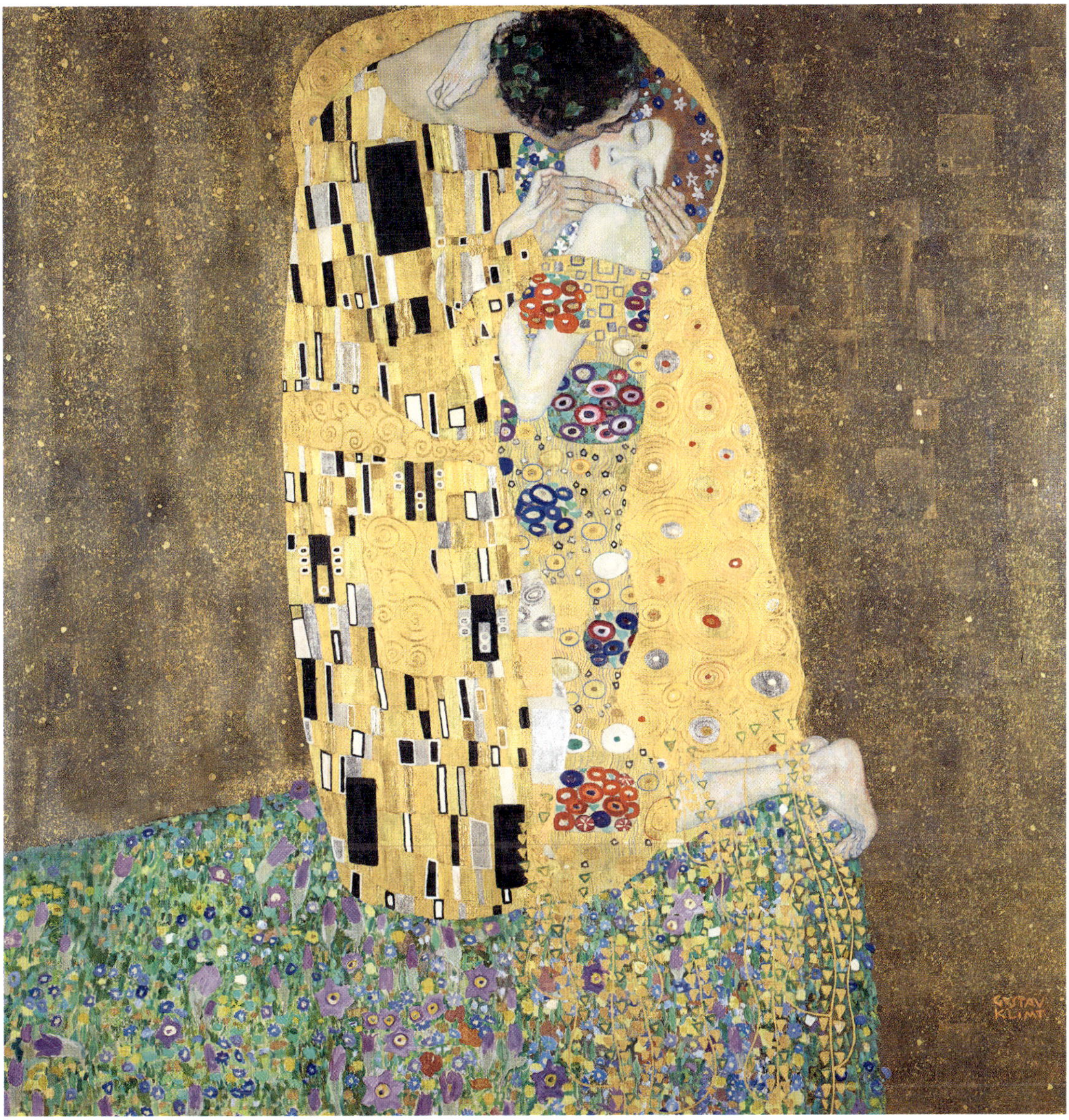

The Kiss, 1908/09, oil and metal leaf on canvas,
180 × 180 cm (70 ⅞ × 70 ⅞ in.), Österreichische Galerie Belvedere, Vienna

GABRIELE MÜNTER
1877–1962

My pictures are all moments of life –
I mean instantaneous visual experiences,
generally noted very rapidly and spontaneously.
When I begin to paint, it's like leaping
suddenly into deep waters,
and I never know beforehand whether I will be able to swim.

GABRIELE MÜNTER, IN CONVERSATION WITH EDOUARD RODITI (1958)

At age twenty-one, Gabriele Münter found herself in a position unusual for most women of her time. She had lost both her parents, but had inherited enough money to live independently and pursue a career in art. By 1898, she had moved to Munich, where she met the people who would have the greatest influence on her career. One was Russian painter Wassily Kandinsky (1866–1944), who first became her tutor at Munich's progressive Phalanx School, and then her artistic and romantic partner for several years. Münter was introduced to the era's most cutting-edge artistic movements, including the intense, saturated colours and simplified forms of Post-Impressionism and Fauvism.

After spending time in Paris with Kandinsky, Münter purchased a house in the small, idyllic Bavarian town of Murnau, on the edge of the Alps south of Munich. It was there that she and Kandinsky, along with two other Russian artist friends, Marianne von Werefkin (1860–1938) and Alexej von Jawlensky (1864–1941), worked together in summer 1908 to develop their artistic practice. Werefkin and Jawlensky, too, were a couple whose relationship had begun as a teacher and student, with the elder Werefkin as teacher. This remarkable gathering saw all four artists learning from and challenging each other in their endeavours. One important result from that summer was Münter's casual portrait of Werefkin and Jawlensky relaxing on a hillside. Landscape and figures are reduced to heavily outlined shapes and vivid greens, yellows and blues. Historians note Werefkin's hat, which resembles a painter's palette, gives the older artist an air of elegant refinement, despite the simplified rendering of her body. *Jawlensky and Werefkin* also evokes a feeling of offhand relaxation, an 'instantaneous visual experience' that somewhat resembles earlier Impressionist art. It is a sunlit world in which artistic innovation is bound up with love and friendship.

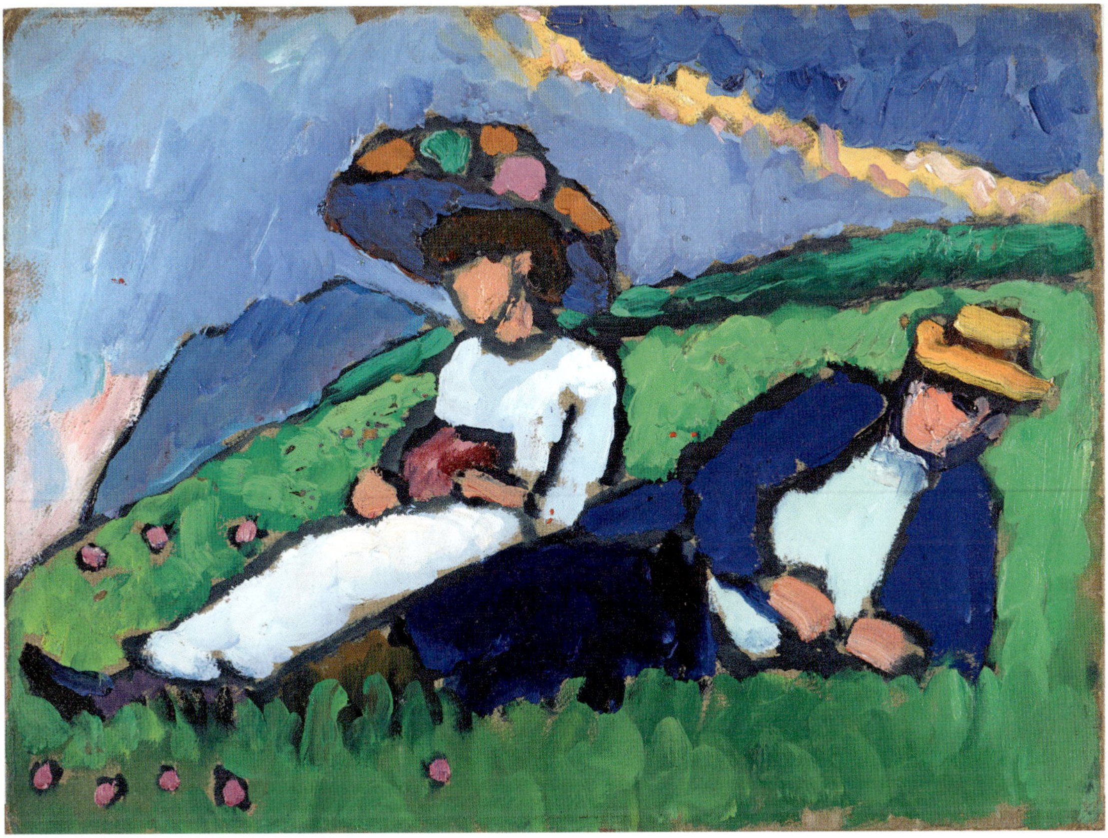

Jawlensky and Werefkin, 1908/09, oil on board,
32.7 × 44.5 cm (12 ⅞ × 17 ½ in.), Städtische Galerie im Lenbachhaus und Kunstbau, Munich

MARC CHAGALL
1887–1985

Her silence is mine. Her eyes, mine.
I feel she has known me always, my childhood, my present life,
my future; as if she were watching over me [...]
I knew this is she, my wife.

MARC CHAGALL DESCRIBING HIS LOVE
FOR HIS WIFE, BELLA ROSENFELD,
IN HIS AUTOBIOGRAPHY *MY LIFE* (1923)

Marc Chagall was born into a modest working-class family near Vitebsk, a small city then in the Russian Empire, and now in Belarus. His Hasidic Jewish parents worked hard to provide for him and his siblings, eventually sending him to school (a privilege not afforded to most Russian Jewish children at the time). Chagall soon discovered an interest in art and, somewhat against his parents' wishes, began attending art school. He also began seeing a young woman in Vitebsk named Basia-Reiza 'Bella' Rosenfeld. Bella Rosenfeld came from a wealthy family in the jewellery trade, and it took Chagall several years to convince her parents that he would make a suitable husband. In 1914, however, an exhibit of his works in Berlin proved highly successful, and Chagall's art began to attract the interest of wealthy clients. Now with a steadier career, he was able to marry his long-time fiancée in 1915.

The marriage was a pivotal moment in Chagall's life, inspiring him to produce many of his most joyous, light-hearted works. Among the best of these is *The Birthday* (1915), which depicts a young couple so in love they are literally floating off the ground. The young man hovers above the woman, his back to the floor and his head twisted around nearly 180 degrees to touch her lips. It is a euphoric expression of desire, which historians argue may be influenced by religious rituals based in the Hasidic Jewish tradition. *The Birthday* also incorporates other elements of Chagall's upbringing in Vitebsk, such as the rich, emotionally resonant colours, the Russian textiles hanging on the wall of the room and the village-like street scene outside the window. Works such as this would play an important role in the development of Surrealism and other avant-garde art movements of the twentieth century.

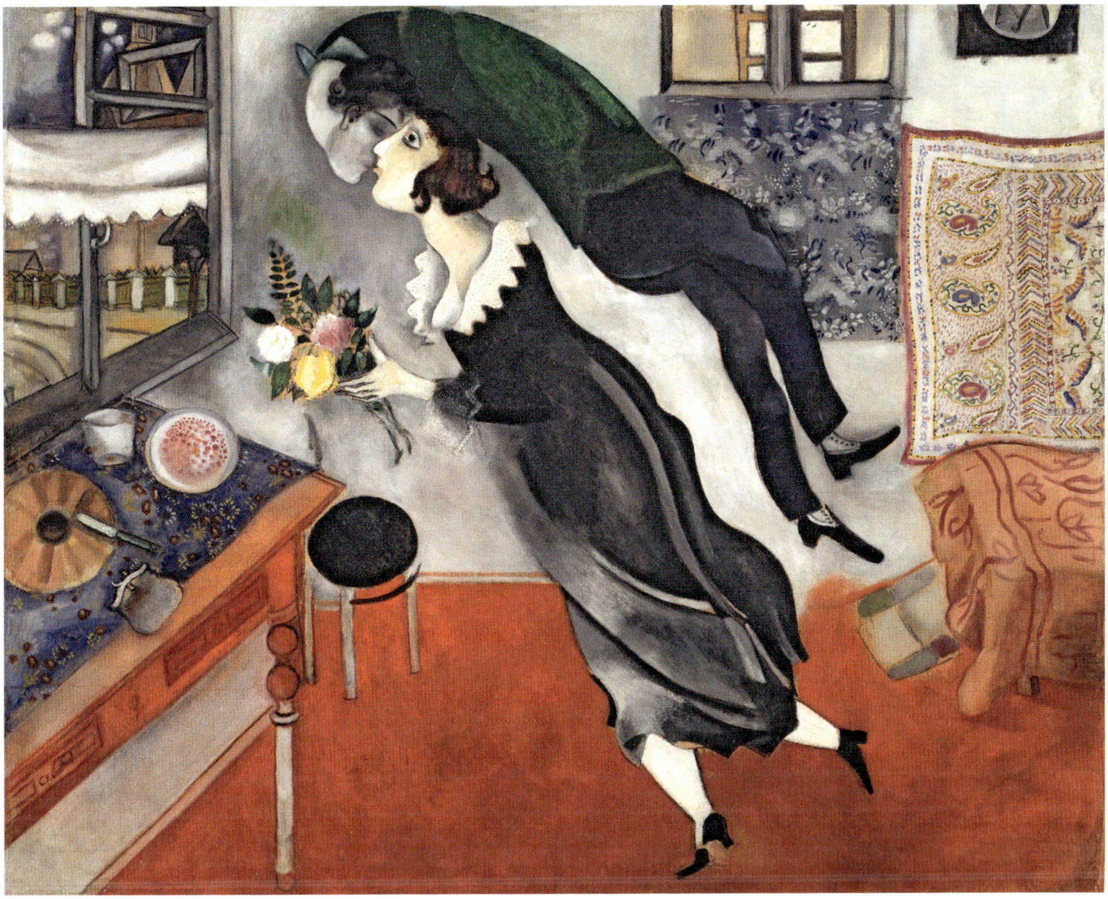

The Birthday, 1915, oil on board,
80.6 × 99.7 cm (31 ¾ × 39 ¼ in.), The Museum of Modern Art (MoMA), New York

MARIANNE VON WEREFKIN
1860–1938

It's been four years now since we've been sleeping side by side.
I've remained a virgin; he's become one again.
Between us sleeps our child – Art.

MARIANNE VON WEREFKIN
ON HER RELATIONSHIP WITH ALEXEJ VON JAWLENSKY,
FROM HER DIARY (1901–1905)

Marianne von Werefkin came from a well-to-do Russian family in Tula, near Moscow. Her mother was an amateur painter, and when the family moved to Saint Petersburg, Werefkin was enrolled in artist Ilya Repin's workshop. There, she met another art student named Alexej von Jawlensky, with whom she would have a long and ultimately tragic relationship. Jawlensky was four years younger than Werefkin, and she would assume the role of his mentor and leading advocate, often at the expense of her own artistic development. In her later journal entries, published as *Letters to an Unknown Man*, Werefkin writes of the emotional struggles she endured in a relationship that avoided – likely in part against her wishes – sexual intimacy.

Strains in the relationship became greater when Jawlensky began having sexual encounters with other women. For a time, however, the two remained partners. Werefkin and Jawlensky would develop their art in Paris and Munich, where they, along with Gabriele Münter and fellow Russian Wassily Kandinsky, would inspire two modern art movements: Der Blaue Reiter (The Blue Rider), with its vibrant colours and references to folk art, as well as abstract art, with its avoidance of natural imagery in favour of abstract shapes and forms. By 1921, however, after the couple had settled in the small Swiss town of Ascona, the cracks in their relationship had become unrepairable, and they formally parted for good.

Drama in her personal life often made its way into Werefkin's art. The small work shown here, *Rapture of Love* from 1917, somewhat recalls Edvard Munch's *The Dance of Life* (p. 79). In it she depicts a couple in several places on the canvas, which, as in Munch's work, likely suggests a single relationship at different points in time. At lower left, the couple engages in a passionate embrace, possibly a reference to the early halcyon days of their partnership. Figures in the background include a woman alienated and standing alone, while the couple in the right foreground, although still embracing, are turned away from each other. They seem resigned to the end of their affair. Unlike *The Dance of Life*, however, Werefkin's image pulsates with 'swirling' forms and colours that seem ablaze – a characteristic that lends the painting its German title *Liebeswirbel* (love swirls). It is a landscape that looks almost like an abstract design; the type of imagery Kandinsky would make famous during this period. *Rapture of Love*, like many of Werefkin's pictures, is a small image modestly pasted on cardboard. But it displays a vigorous, emotional energy – one that helped break apart the old traditions of painting.

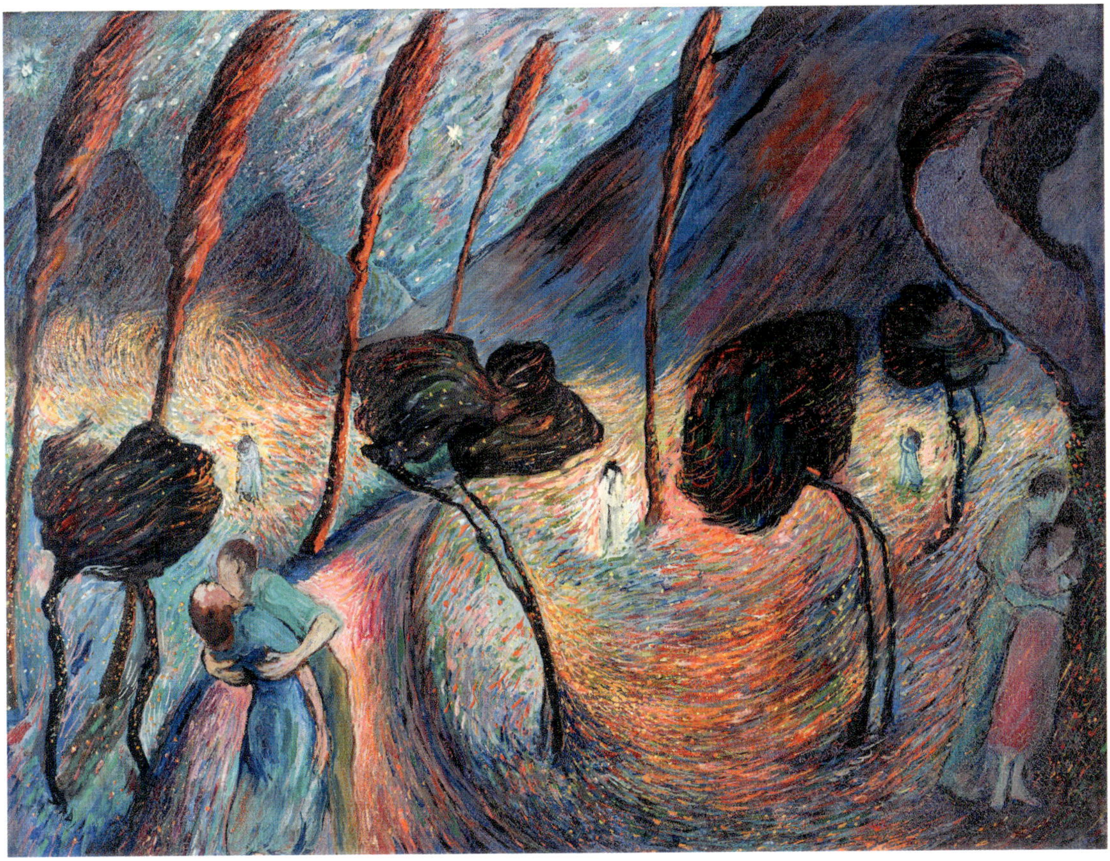

Rapture of Love, c. 1917, tempera on paper mounted on board,
45.5 × 60 cm (17 ⅞ × 23 ⅝ in.), Kunsthaus Zürich, permanent loan of Dr Peter Diego Hagmann

PABLO PICASSO
1881–1973

You can go on talking about love,
but there comes a moment when it turns sour,
and that's when you have to pay the laundry bill.

PABLO PICASSO, RECOUNTED IN THE MEMOIRS OF HIS LOVER GENEVIÈVE LAPORTE (1973)

World War I (1914–1918) had a devastating impact in Europe. The massive loss of life, often with technologically advanced weaponry, and the sometimes-unclear motives underlying the war, made many Europeans distrust notions of 'progress' and 'improvement' that had been popular since the Industrial Revolution. This growing cynicism was especially prevalent among artists, many of whom had been developing radical new styles of 'progressive' art. Some of these artists now began to look backwards in time for new inspiration: a so-called 'return to order'.

Spanish-born artist Pablo Picasso had been at the forefront of the avant-garde art revolution. He had helped develop the first truly modern style of the twentieth century, Cubism; and he made radical experiments with collage and sculpture as well. In many of his works, human forms appeared broken apart and reassembled. But Picasso's art began to change dramatically as the war progressed. While traveling to Italy in 1917, to design sets and costumes for a ballet, Picasso explored the great collections of Renaissance and Baroque art in Rome, Florence and Naples. These classic masterpieces, along with his emotional fatigue over the war, led Picasso to begin his 'neoclassical' period, in which he explored ways of merging modern styles with traditional figural painting.

One good example of Picasso's neoclassical art is shown here. Titled *The Lovers*, it depicts a tender moment between a young man and woman. The man has his right arm around the woman's shoulder, while holding her left hand with his own. He stares intently at her, possibly in the act of declaring love, while she casts her eyes slightly downwards. Gone are the jagged Cubist experiments of Picasso's earlier work, now replaced by realistic bodies with distinctively Mediterranean features. The slightly triangular composition, too, has a quality reminiscent of old masters such as Raphael. Yet *The Lovers* remains a work of modernism. Picasso avoids the use of traditional shading, rendering the couple with broad patches of strong colour and defined black outlines. The overall space, as well, is flat and non-realistic. It is an artistic union of ancient and modern – and a call for love in an era torn by conflict.

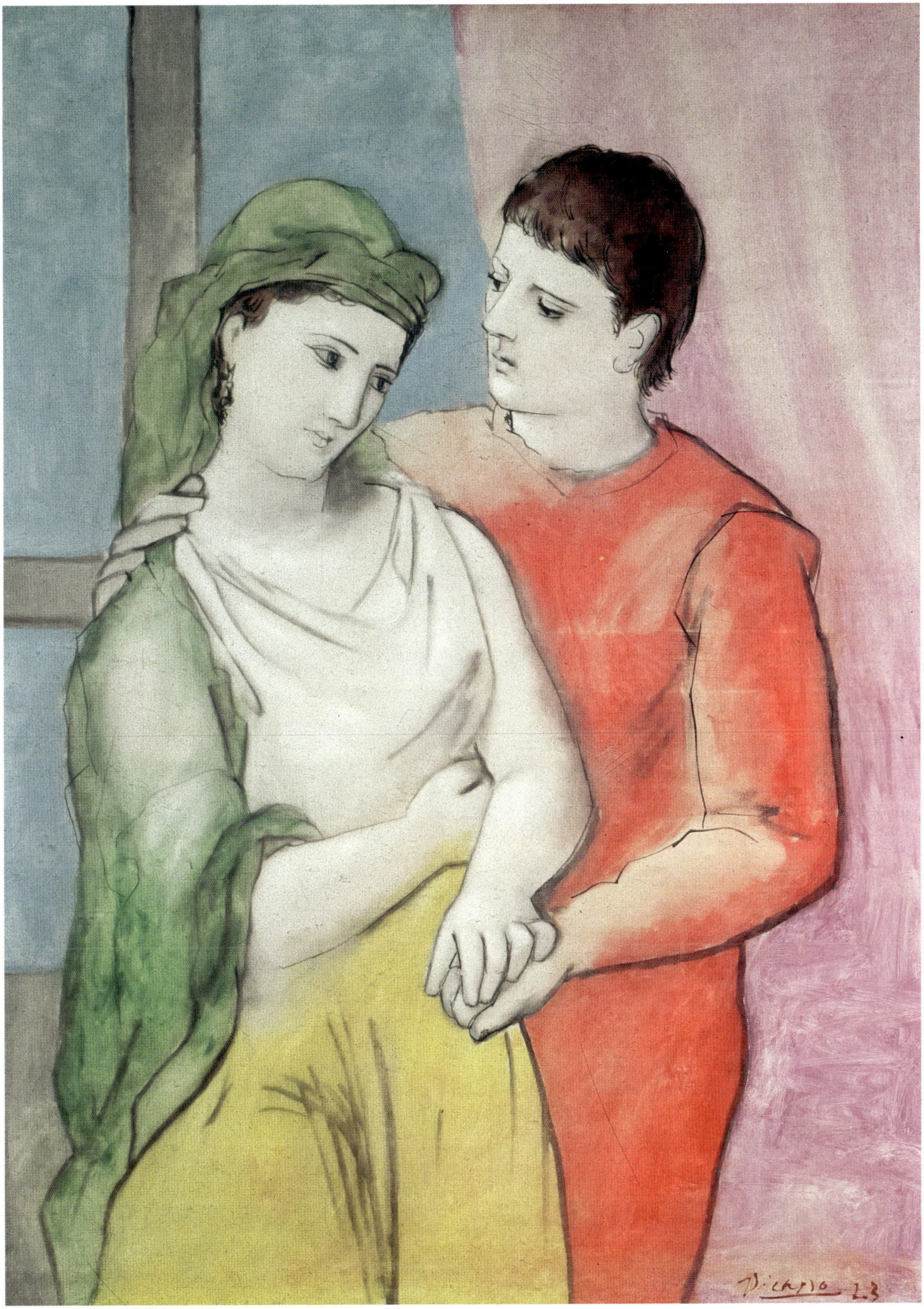

The Lovers, 1923, oil on linen,
130.2 × 97.2 cm (51 ¼ × 38 ¼ in.), National Gallery of Art, Washington, DC

PAUL KLEE
1879–1940

The power of creativity cannot be named.
It remains mysterious to the end. [...]
We ourselves, down to the smallest part of us,
are charged with this power.
We cannot state its essence but we can,
in certain measure, move towards its source.
In any case we must reveal this power in its functions
just as it is revealed to us.

PAUL KLEE, 'THE CONCEPT OF ARTISTIC CREATION',
FROM A LECTURE AT THE BAUHAUS (c. 1920–1925)

For Paul Klee, love and creation were 'mysterious' realities that an artist had the power to reveal, at least in part. He worked with a variety of twentieth-century artists, including Der Blaue Reiter (The Blue Rider) group in Germany, and his own idiosyncratic style grew out of various art movements, such as Cubism and Expressionism. But as beloved as his own art may be, Klee is often best remembered as a teacher at the Bauhaus. This school in Germany, which combined the teaching of fine art with modern design, fostered a wide range of creative pursuits – from painters to architects to designers of household goods. Klee taught his pupils how simplified shapes, colours and lines could express deeper realities, and that abstract art could be just as potent emotionally as traditional realism.

In his watercolour *Eros*, from 1923, we can see both Klee the artist and Klee the teacher at work. Concepts of love and union are reduced to simple triangles and arrows. The painting focuses on a single point where the upward triangles and downward triangles meet. Klee often referred to 'male' and 'female' as opposite forces in art, and here we see a merging of opposite 'male' and 'female' shapes – reminiscent of the sexual merging of man and woman. This artistic union of geometric forms is enhanced by Klee's subtly gradated colours, which also merge at the same place. Created using watercolour and gouache, the colours give his work a shimmering, mystical quality. It is the type of image Klee used to instruct his students on the value of abstract form and design. It is also a work that, for modern-day viewers, can capture some of the mysteries of love and spiritual union.

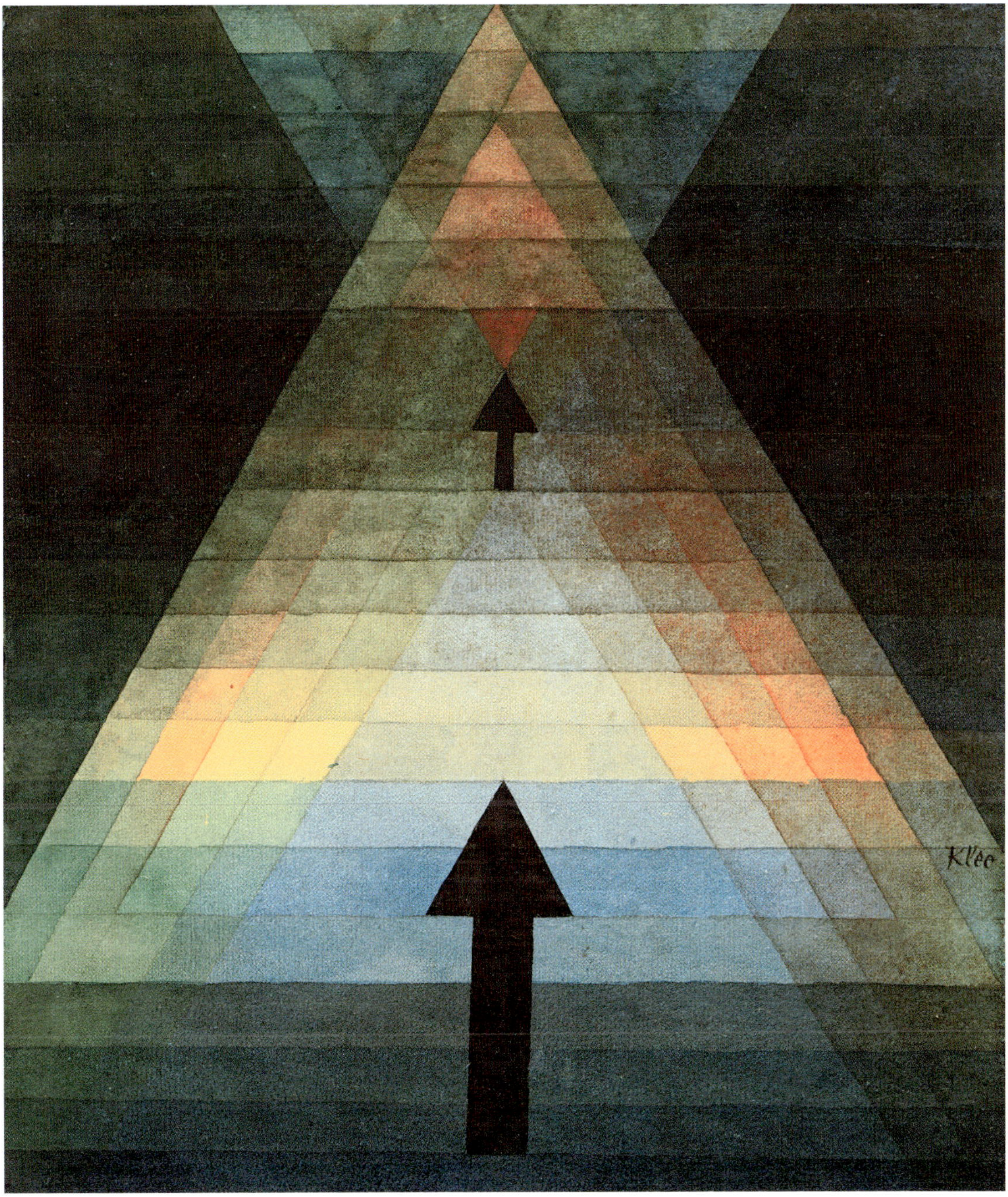

Eros, 1923, watercolour, gouache and pencil on paper, cut and recombined,
strip on the bottom in watercolour and pen, bordered in gouache and pen,
mounted on board, 33.3 × 24.5 cm (13 ⅛ × 9 ⅝ in.), Museum Rosengart Collection, Lucerne

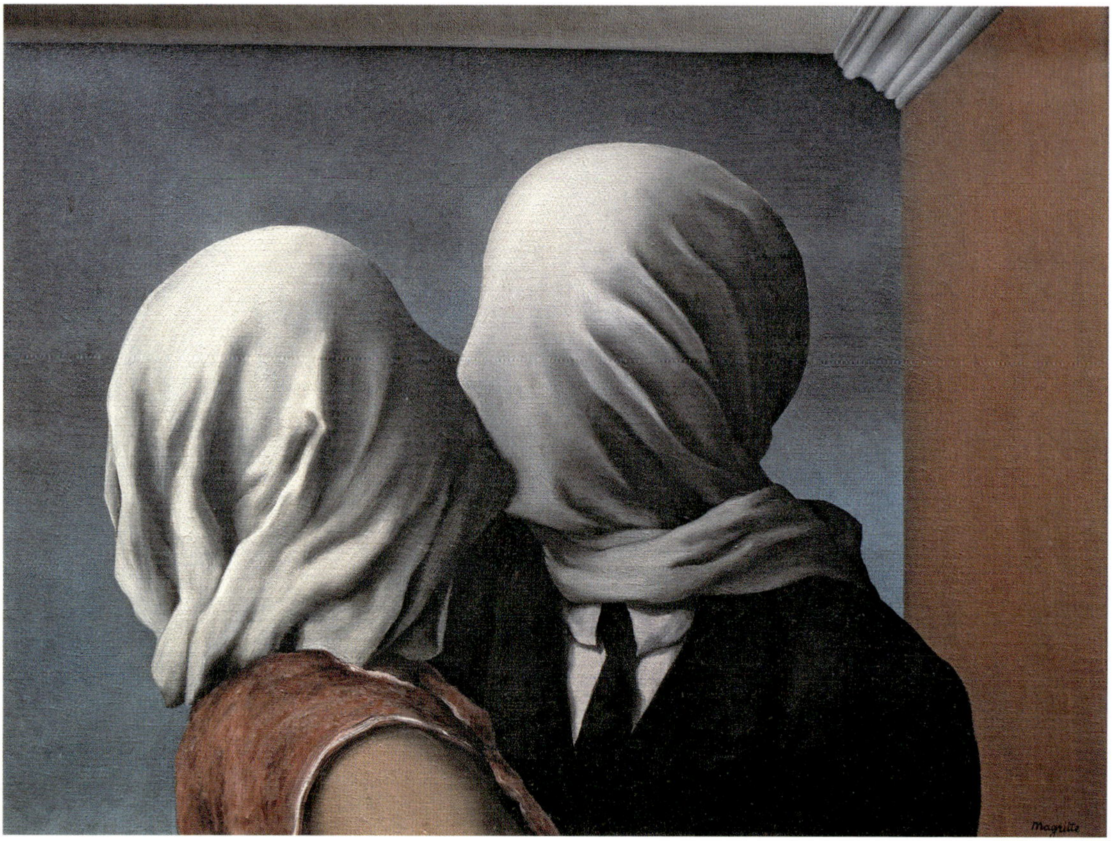

The Lovers, 1928, oil on canvas,
54 × 73.4 cm (21 ¼ × 28 ⅞ in.), The Museum of Modern Art (MoMA), New York

RENÉ MAGRITTE
1898–1967

My painting[s ...] evoke mystery and, indeed, when one sees one of my pictures, one asks oneself the simple question ' What does that mean?' It does not mean anything, because mystery means nothing either, it is unknowable.

RENÉ MAGRITTE (c. 1960)

Belgian artist René Magritte was a leader of the Surrealist movement, a style of art known for combining realism with odd, unexplained juxtapositions. Magritte developed his style after experiencing traumatic moments in his childhood. His mother, Régina, committed suicide by drowning when René was only fourteen. The young Magritte watched as his mother's dead body was dragged out of the river with her nightgown covering her face. As an adult, he would make a number of paintings, including *The Lovers*, with figures whose faces are obscured by fabric. Art critics have often tried to find meaning in these works by linking them with Magritte's mother's death, but Magritte himself rejected the idea of 'meaning' in his art.

The Lovers now hangs in New York's Museum of Modern Art (MoMA), one of four 'Lovers' paintings that Magritte created in 1928. It shows a couple from the shoulders up, embracing. The positioning of the bodies and heads suggests a level of passion between the two individuals – a passion deliberately obscured by the cloth covering their faces and hiding their facial expressions. Despite Magritte's insistence that this and other works have no real meaning, art historians and viewers have offered many ways of interpreting *The Lovers*. Does the work suggest an artist plagued by unrequited love? Does it reflect a sense of isolation and estrangement that many Europeans felt after 1918 and the end of the First World War? Magritte's art is meant to raise more questions than answers.

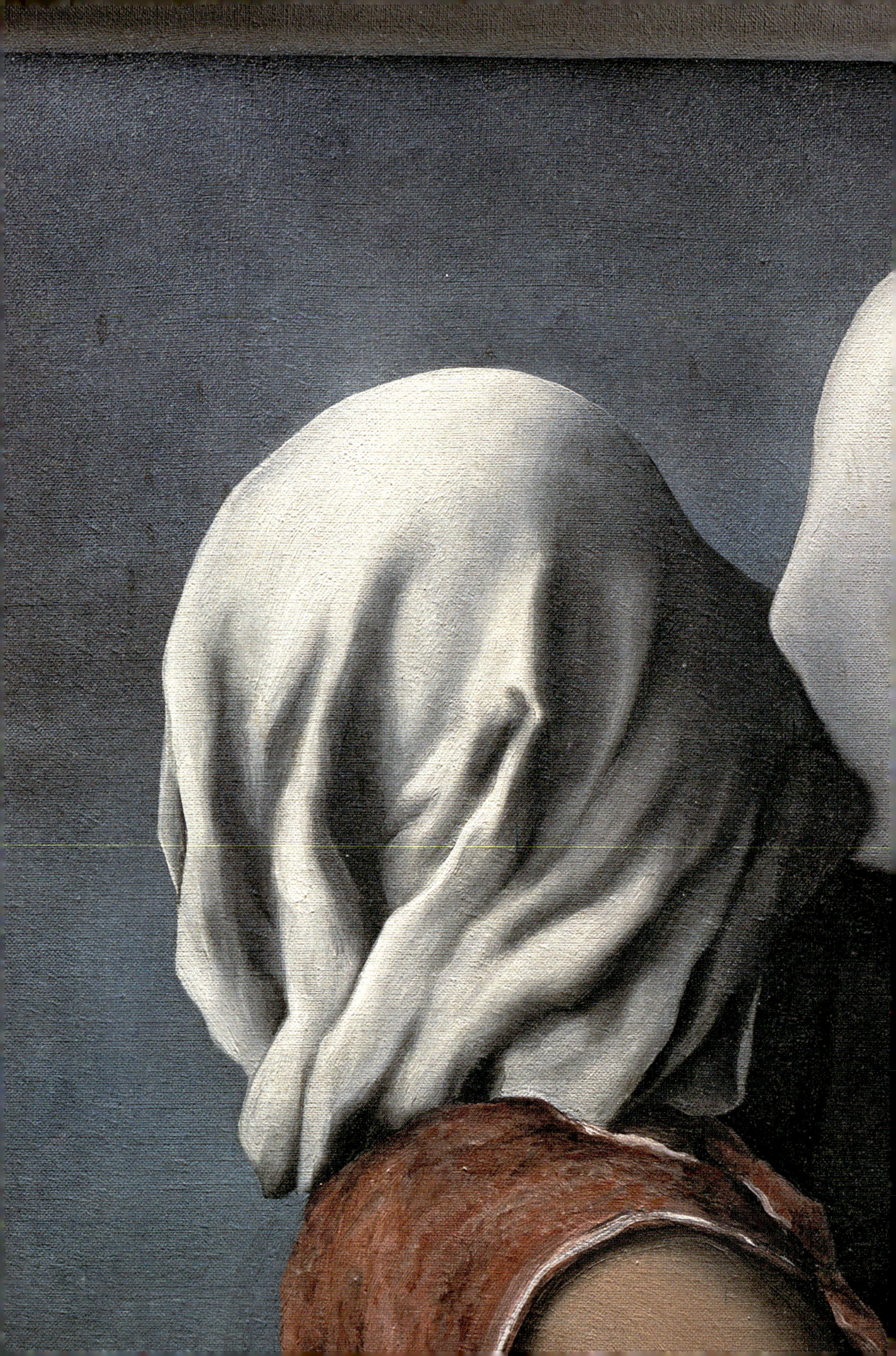

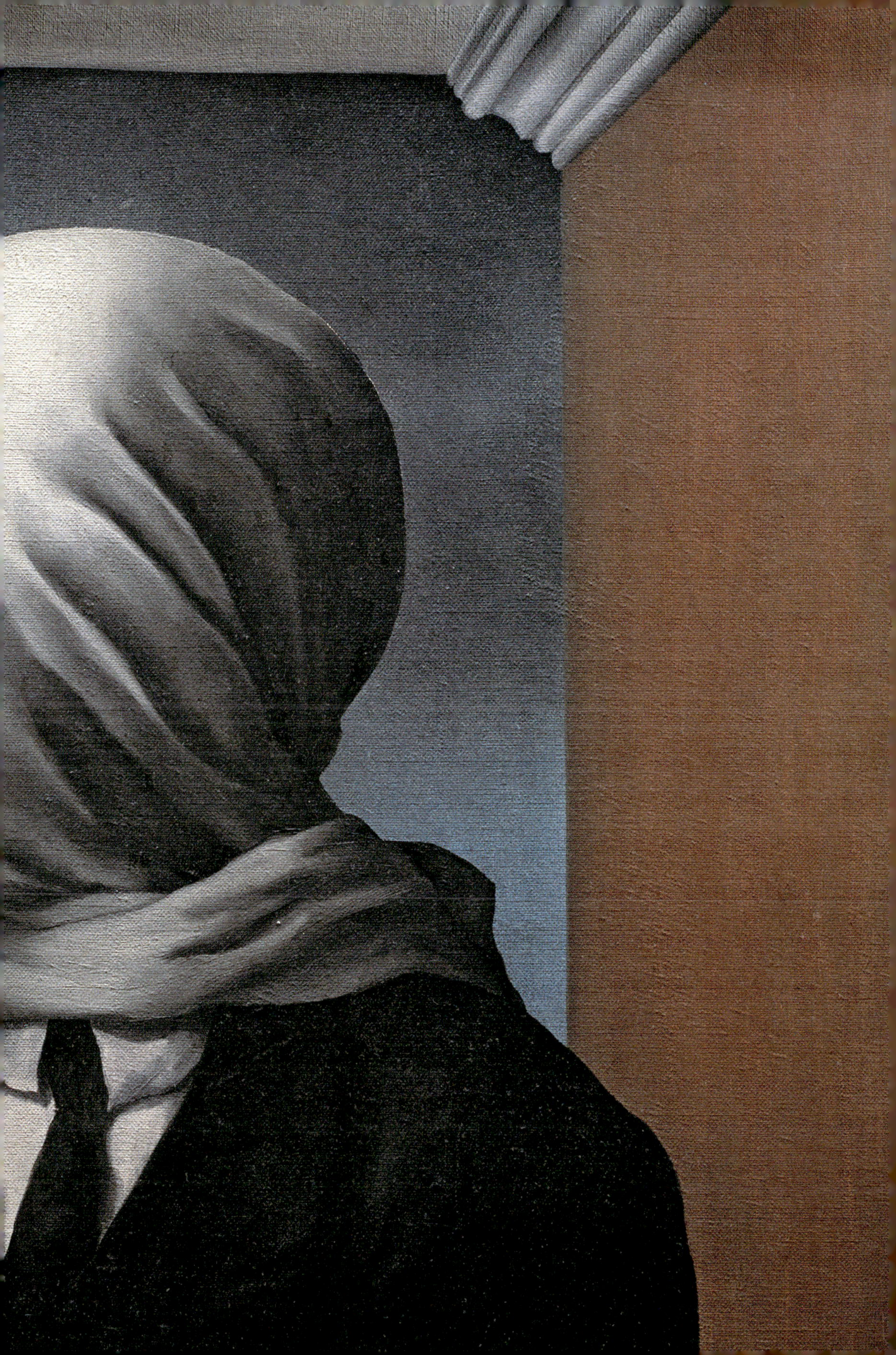

GRANT WOOD
1891–1942

These are types of people I have known all my life.
I tried to characterize them truthfully –
to make them more like themselves than they were in actual life.
They had their bad points […]
but to me they were basically good and solid people.
I had no intention of holding them up to ridicule.

GRANT WOOD, IN DEFENCE OF HIS PAINTING,
TO THE *CEDAR RAPIDS GAZETTE* (1942)

In summer 1930, American artist Grant Wood was visiting friends in the small Midwestern town of Eldon, in southern Iowa. While there, an old wood-frame farmhouse caught his eye. The home had been built in the 1880s, and it featured a distinctive gothic window above a simple porch. Grant Wood had developed a painting style that sought to describe the people and landscape of Iowa, his home state; and the Eldon farmhouse (known as the Dibble House, after its builder, Charles A. Dibble, 1836–1923) became the inspiration for an unusual double 'portrait'. Wood would call the painting *American Gothic*, in part as a way of describing the revival style of this house.

The couple portrayed in *American Gothic*, however, never lived in the house. Instead, Wood used 'models' from his own hometown as inspiration. The woman was based on Wood's sister, Nan Wood Graham, and the man on his family dentist, Dr Byron McKeeby. Grant Wood wanted to present a couple that people might recognize as 'typical' rural Midwesterners. He gave them stern faces and old-fashioned clothing, as well as an antique, three-pronged pitchfork, which contemporary farmers in Iowa had not been using for decades.

Wood's painting soon drew widespread attention and notoriety in the press. The *Des Moines Sunday Register* printed an image of the painting under the title 'An Iowa Farmer and His Wife'. But many of the early reviews and comments were not positive. Critics saw the painting as disrespectful, a satire of provincial America. They thought Wood's portrayal made the couple look stiff, culturally backward, uneducated and a bit sanctimonious. The artist, however, assured his naysayers that the work was not a parody, but a portrait of 'good, solid people'. He also revealed that the couple was not intended to be a man and wife, but a man and his daughter. For Wood, *American Gothic* exemplified the strong, stern family bonds (bonds of love and duty) that characterized life in rural America. Today, the work has become an iconic American image – widely reproduced in ways that are both admiring and satirical.

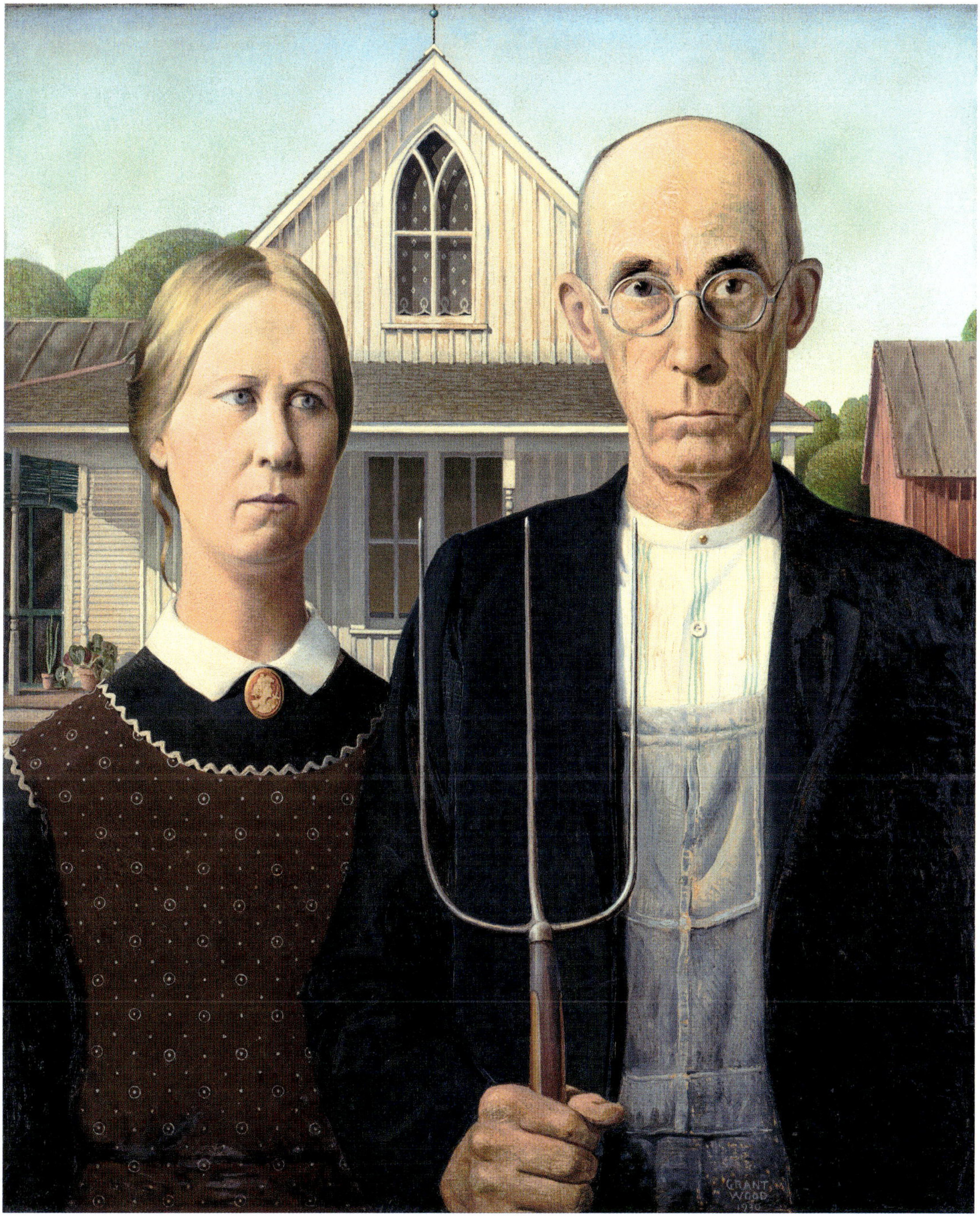

American Gothic, 1930, oil on Beaverboard,
78 × 65.3 cm (30 ¾ × 25 ¾ in.), The Art Institute of Chicago

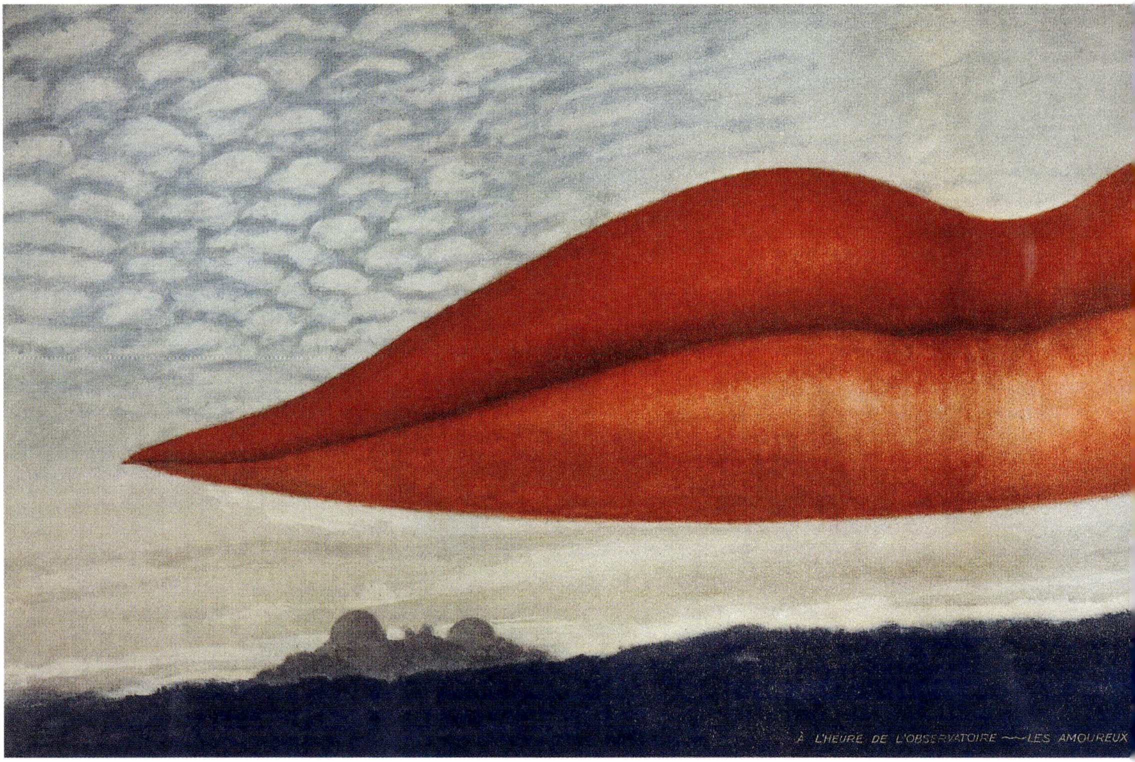

MAN RAY
1890–1976

Lips of sun, you attract me ceaselessly,
and in this moment before wakening,
when I detach myself from my body – I am weightless –
I join you again in the neutral light and in the empty space,
and, sole reality, I kiss you with all that still remains of me:
my own lips.

MAN RAY, 'OBSERVATORY TIME … THE LOVERS' (1935)

American artist Man Ray was born Emmanuel Radnitzky in Philadelphia. The son of Russian Jewish immigrants, he began to explore modern art seriously after 1912, when he enrolled in New York's radical Ferrer Modern School. Man Ray soon made contacts with the most progressive artists of his day, including Marcel Duchamp (1887–1968) and Salvador Dalí (1904–1989), and he developed a style of painting and photography that featured ordinary objects – or combinations of objects – in unusual positions or lighting.

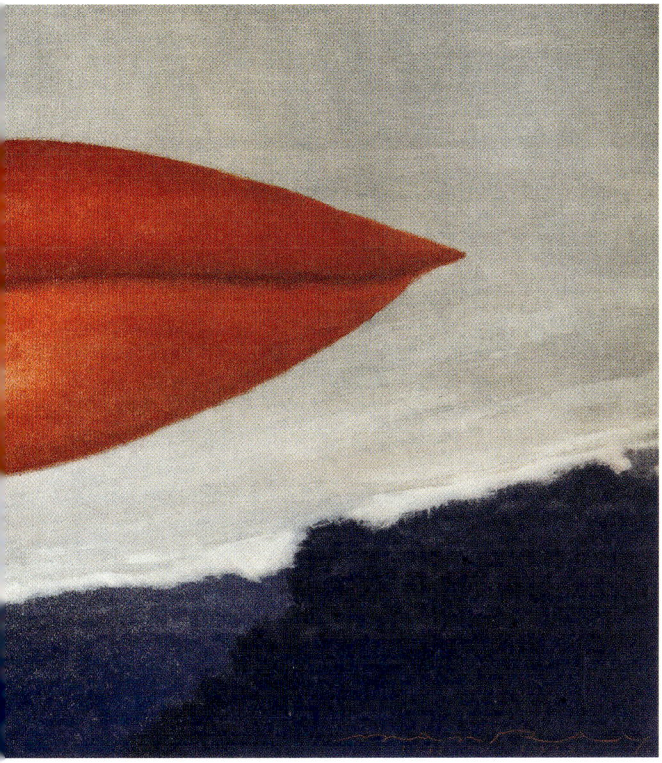

His images gave the objects a sometimes eerie or provocative appearance, inspiring emotions in the viewer far removed from the objects' ordinary uses. Such art helped spearhead a movement known as Surrealism.

The oil painting known in English as *Observatory Time – The Lovers*, upon which the lithograph shown here is based, has become a Surrealist icon. Spreading above a realistically detailed landscape are a huge pair of lips. Man Ray positions the lips to make them look like an integral part of the cloud-dotted sky; as though the sky itself made up the lower part of a human face. One also gets the sense that lips and sky could open up and engulf the viewer completely. Art critics have interpreted the work as Man Ray's response to a difficult break-up with Lee Miller (1907–1977), his photography assistant and lover from 1929 to 1932. Miller, an important photographer in her own right, was a strong-willed woman, and the couple's parting may have been emotionally traumatic. Even Man Ray's own writing on the picture suggests the all-encompassing nature of these lips – a symbol of his continuing romantic obsession with his former lover. It was an affair that 'swallowed' him whole emotionally, those 'lips of sun'.

À l'heure de l'observatoire – Les amoureux (Observatory Time – The Lovers), 1932–1934/1970, lithograph, 63 × 103 cm (24 ¾ × 40 ½ in.)

FRIDA KAHLO
1907–1954

[...] he says he loves me more than any other girl. I am very happy.

FRIDA KAHLO ON HER REMARRIAGE TO DIEGO RIVERA, IN A LETTER TO FRIEND SIGMUND FIRESTONE (1940)

Born in the Mexico City neighbourhood of Coyoacán, Frida Kahlo was the daughter of a German-born father and a mother whose ancestry was both Spanish and Purépecha (an Indigenous people of western Mexico). After suffering polio as a child, and then a disastrous accident with a bus at age eighteen, Kahlo spent much of her adult life in severe pain. Her disabilities, however, did not prevent her from living a remarkably full life. Kahlo married Diego Rivera (1886–1957), the great Mexican muralist, in 1929, and the two had an often-stormy relationship. Infidelities committed by both partners led to separation and a divorce in 1939, but they could never break permanently with each other, and they married again in 1940 – a union that would last until Kahlo's death.

Kahlo's health deteriorated rapidly over the course of her short life, and much of her art was created in her bedroom. A mirror had been placed above her bed so she could study and paint her own face. Much of Kahlo's art, in fact, focuses on her own self-portrait, as well as her love for both Rivera and her indigenous Mexican heritage. The work entitled *Self-Portrait as a Tehuana* (also known as *Diego on My Mind*) captures all three of these influences. Here we see Kahlo's face almost engulfed by the traditional Tehuana lace headdress (or *resplandor*) of the Zapotec culture of southern Mexico; while her 'thoughts' of Rivera are embodied by a tiny portrait of Diego placed on her forehead. Kahlo also displays another love – her love of nature – by a bouquet of flowers and leaves on her head, which have roots that extend outwards like a web to the edges of the painting. All of this imagery surrounds the face of the artist, portrayed with a mixture of fierceness and vulnerability. For Kahlo, married love seems to have been intertwined with the love of her heritage and of the natural world around her.

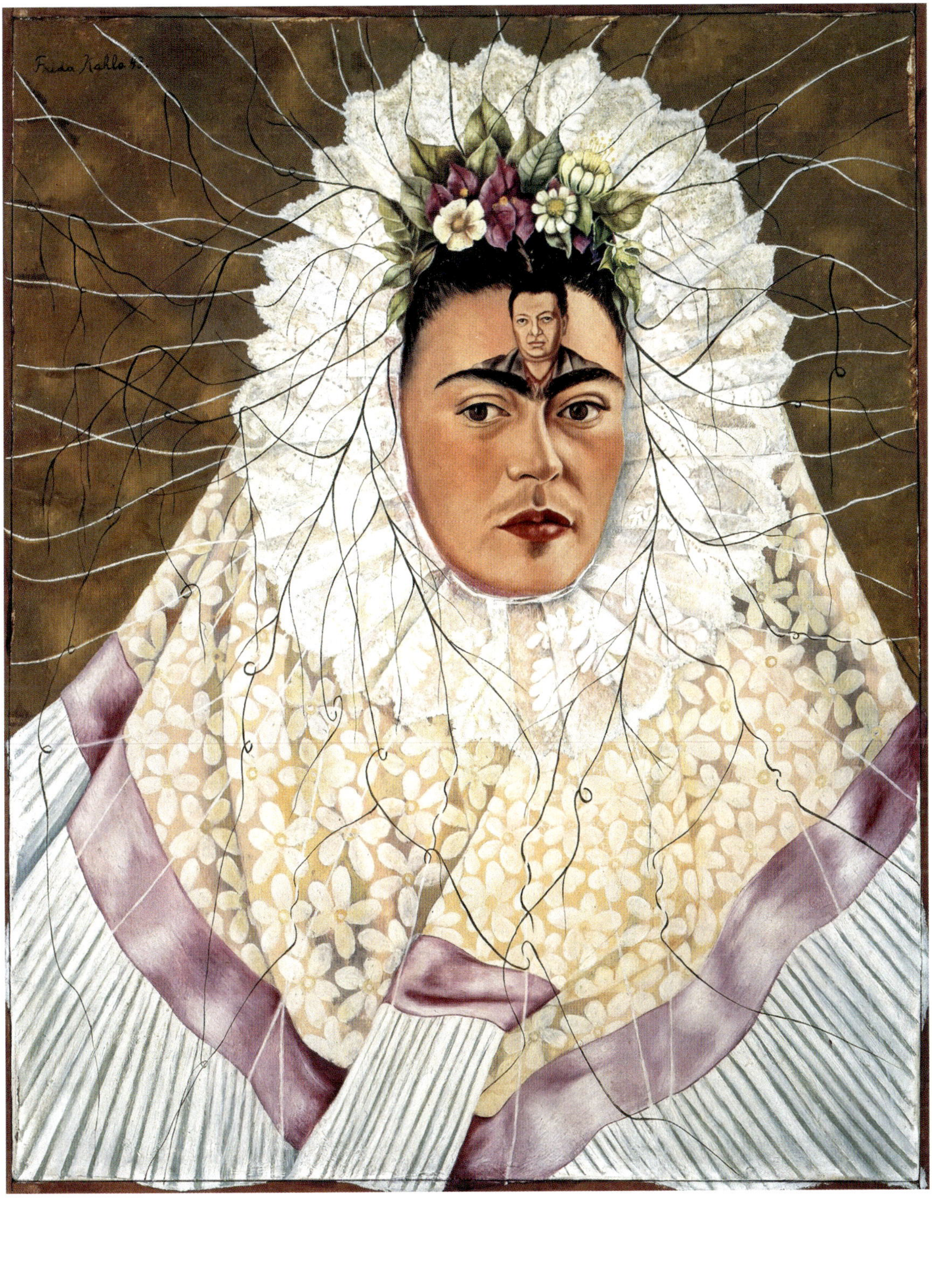

Self-Portrait as a Tehuana (Diego on My Mind), 1943, oil on Masonite,
75.9 × 61 cm (29 ⅞ × 24 in.), Colección Gelman Santander, Faro Santander

GERHARD RICHTER
born 1932

I wanted to show the things that are always overlooked in a little snapshot. Snapshots are not thought of as art, but if they are transported into art, they take on a dignity and they are regarded.

GERHARD RICHTER, IN CONVERSATION WITH WOLFGANG PEHNT (1989)

Love seems out of reach in this photo-painting by Gerhard Richter, the dean of contemporary German artists. Richter has been experimenting with his craft for nearly seven decades. Born in Dresden, in the last year of the Weimar Republic, he grew up in a Germany marked by dictatorship and war, and came of age in divided postwar Europe, on the communist eastern side. Richter's early training led him to produce murals and other works of Socialist Realism, the officially sanctioned traditional style of the Soviet Bloc. Everything changed for him, however, in 1961, when he and his wife fled East Germany for the western city of Düsseldorf. There, Richter immersed himself in the techniques and ideas of modernist and post-modernist art.

His personal style first emerged during the 1960s with his photo-paintings. Using blurred, black-and-white snapshots, Richter painstakingly recreated them with oil on canvas. The artist chose snapshot images from a large number he had collected. Most of these photos contained seemingly unimportant or random moments. But as Richter said in a later interview, they could acquire a certain 'dignity' when 'transported' into the realm of art. The image shown here, first painted in 1966, depicts a young couple in the woods. Dressed in the fashion of the time, with boots and patterned minidress, the woman is in the midst of an embrace with her 'lover'. It is a blurry, fleeting image of an anonymous couple, one where the viewer is kept emotionally distant. But it also engages us, as though we were frustrated voyeurs who cannot quite make out what we are seeing. In the years since its initial exhibition, *Lovers in the Forest* has come full circle, so to speak. A popular image for art collectors, it has been reproduced and sold commercially as a lithograph poster. Thus the old snapshot has been transformed once again – from a painting back to a printed image.

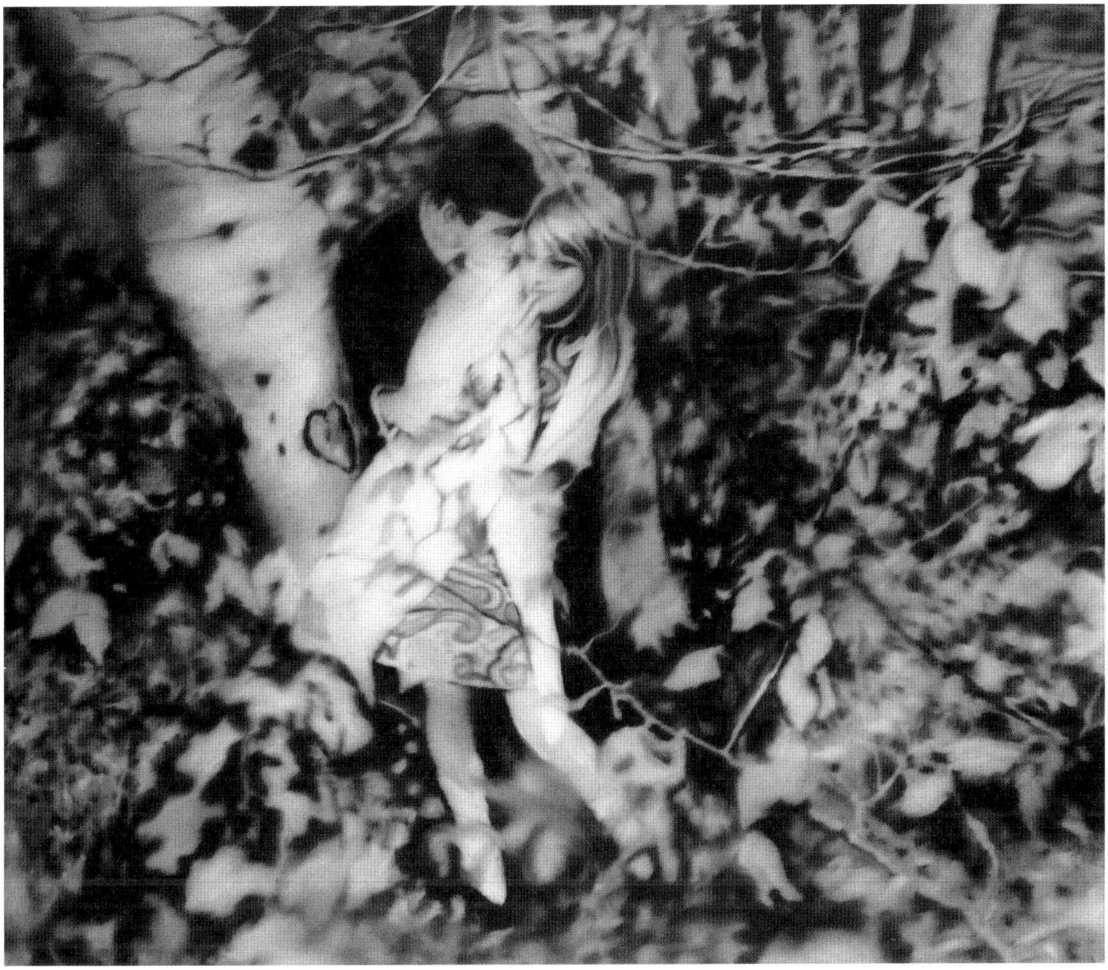

Lovers in the Forest, 1966, oil on canvas,
170 × 200 cm (66 ⅞ × 78 ¾ in.), Private Collection

ROBERT INDIANA
1928–2018

Everybody knows my LOVE,
but they don't have the slightest idea what I look like.
I'm practically anonymous.

ROBERT INDIANA, IN CONVERSATION
WITH JEFF GOLDBERG (1976)

American artist Robert Indiana's *LOVE* is more than an artwork; it is an image instantly recognized by millions in the United States and elsewhere. The work began in 1964 as a postcard – first for Indiana's friends and then for the Christmas season at New York's Museum of Modern Art (MoMA). The success of Indiana's postcards led to more elaborate versions of the image, from paintings to screenprints to monumental sculptures. Eventually, the work made a splash in the commercial world, where it was used on postage stamps, magazine advertisements and posters. *LOVE*'s widespread appeal made it a visual icon of the 1960s and 1970s, an era when ideas about love and sex were becoming more progressive. This popularity eventually outstripped – and even subsumed – the fame of its maker. Today, few people have, as Indiana said, 'the slightest idea' who created the work.

Robert Indiana (born Robert Clark) adopted his professional name after his home state, and he often described his art as autobiographical. When talking about the genesis of *LOVE*, he spoke of his childhood: 'my father worked for Phillips 66, when all Phillips 66 gas stations were red and green: the pumps, the uniforms, the oil cans. [...] I would see, practically every day of my young life, a huge Phillips 66 sign. So it is the red and green of that sign against the blue Hoosier sky. The blue in the *LOVE* is cerulean. Therefore my *LOVE* is a homage to my father.'

Indiana had been making art inspired by traditional signage since the 1950s. These works featured numbers, letters and words in tight geometrical arrangements. In *LOVE*, the 'LO' and 'VE' are placed on separate lines to form a square, with the hard-edged letters touching each other and extending to the borders of the picture. This rigid geometry, however, is broken up by the letter 'O', which is placed at an angle and gives the image a suggestive quality. Also suggestive is the bold Didone typeface, with its subtle curves, distinctive serifs as well as the negative spaces within and in between the letters. In the screenprint version of *LOVE* shown here, these shapes and spaces, as well as the colour scheme, create a slight optical illusion; a perception of movement and instability. *LOVE*'s aesthetic qualities have led to debates among art critics over how to define or categorize the work. The piece also reveals the power that 'love' – even the word itself – continues to have in our culture.

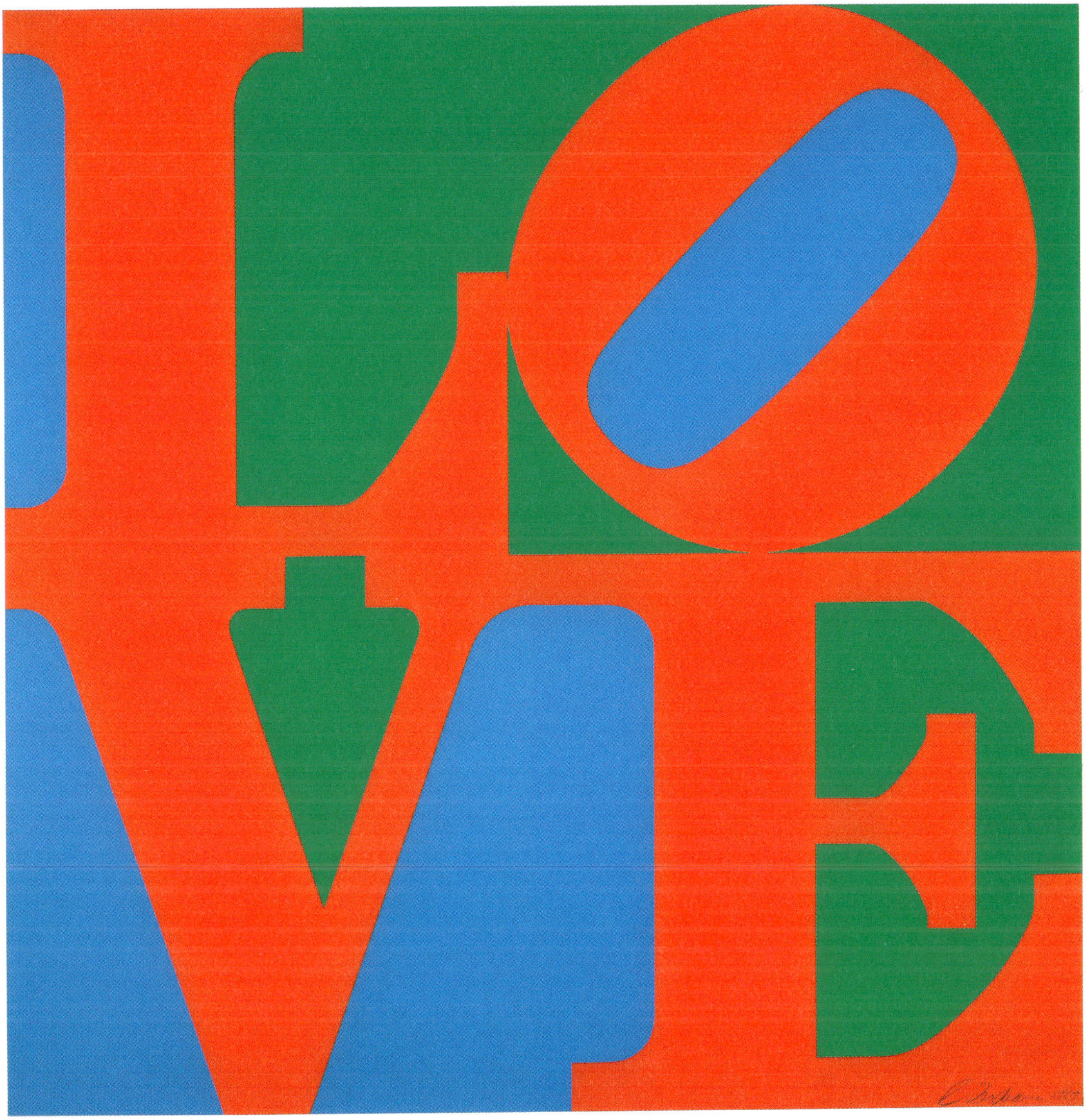

LOVE, 1967, screenprint,
86.3 × 86.3 cm (34 × 34 in.), The Museum of Modern Art (MoMA), New York

KEITH HARING
1958–1990

I've always believed that you live life as fully and as completely as you can – and you deal with the future as it comes to you.

KEITH HARING, IN CONVERSATION WITH JOHN GRUEN (1990)

In 1969, riots at the Stonewall Inn in New York saw LGBTQ people fighting back against a police raid. Such raids were common at a time when many municipalities in the United States criminalized gay and lesbian activity. But the events at Stonewall began to change how people thought of the LGBTQ community, and it helped launch the gay rights movement. Over the following decades, this movement would gain steam, partly through the visibility of work by artists like Keith Haring.

Haring grew up in a conservative family in Kutztown, a small community in Pennsylvania. An early love of cartoons led him to study art, and in 1978, he moved to New York. Haring quickly became immersed in the city's growing community of street artists. New York's subways were getting rid of old advertisements on the walls of their stations, and artists took advantage of the empty space to make graffiti paintings where the ads had once been. Haring began developing his signature style, which owed much to graphic art, on these underground 'canvasses'. It would mark the beginning of his rapid rise to prominence.

Be Mine represents the kind of work that made Haring famous. It features his signature cartoon figures, produced here in silkscreen ink and rendered with thick black outlines. It also includes his signature heart, which, with its saturated red centre, offers the work's only element of colour. Despite the pared-down, almost humorous, simplicity of the image, *Be Mine* makes a potent statement of love and acceptance. The gender of the figures is left intentionally vague, suggesting that intimate love should be open to all couples, regardless of sexuality. Haring depicts the figures as having a kind of silent conversation, with the right-hand individual putting an arm around the other, more apprehensive, figure. It is a gesture that seems designed to dispel fear and to encourage the search for one's true desires in love and relationships.

Works such as *Be Mine*, with their light-hearted touch, helped pave the way for an acceptance of gay marriage and other aspects of LGBTQ life in broader society. Haring, sadly, would not survive to see these cultural advances. He died of AIDS-related complications in 1990, at age thirty-one.

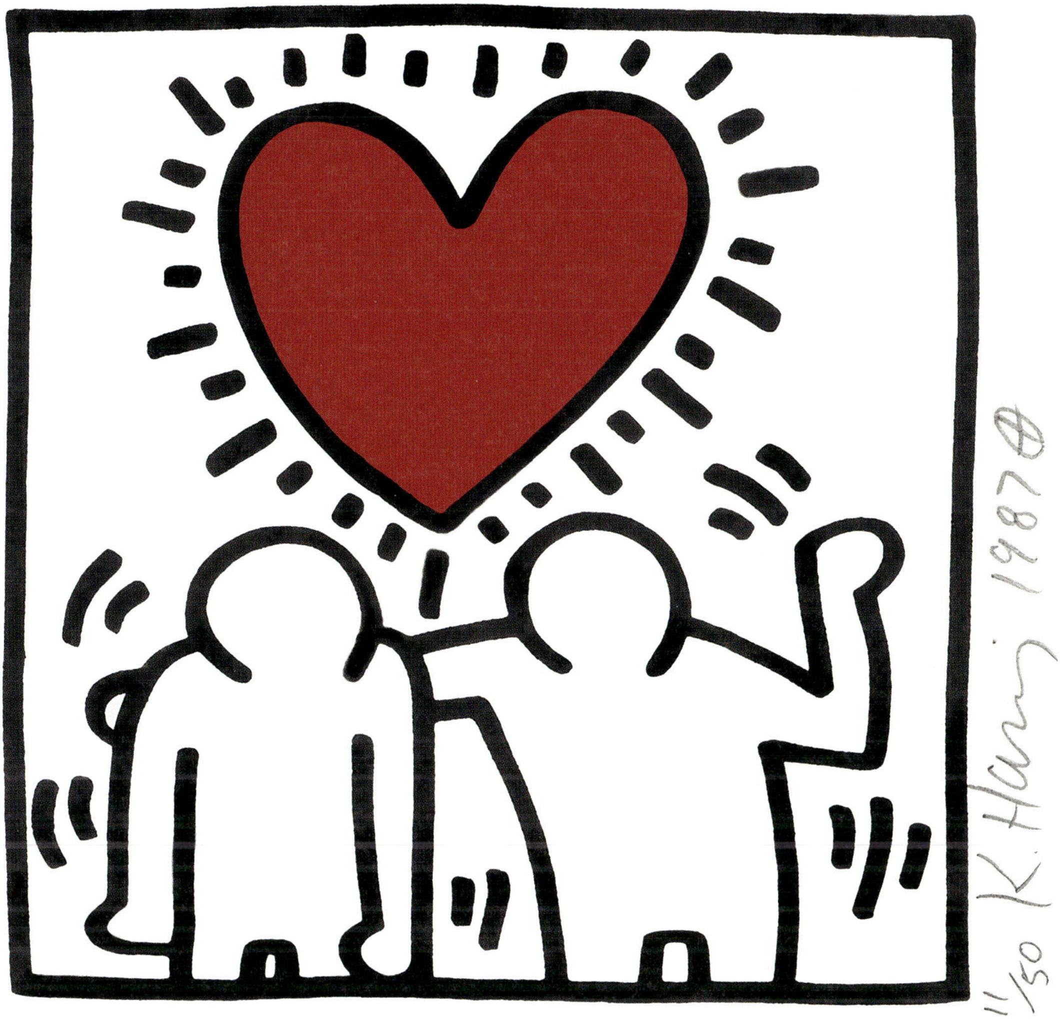

Untitled (Be Mine), 1987, silkscreen ink on paper, no. 11 of an edition of 50,
15.2 × 15.2 cm (6 × 6 in.), Private Collection

MARINA ABRAMOVIĆ

born 1946

> *At a chosen location*
> *We walked the entire length of the Great Wall of China.*
> *We started on 30 March 1988.*
> *[...] After we both continuously walked for 90 days,*
> *we met at Er Lang Shan, in Shen Mu, Shaanxi province.*
> *We each took a 2,000 kilometre walk to say goodbye.*

MARINA ABRAMOVIĆ,
ARTIST STATEMENT FOR *THE LOVERS* (1988)

In 1980, Serbian-born performance artist Marina Abramović and her then-partner, German-born artist Ulay (Frank Uwe Laysiepen, 1943–2020), spent time in the forbidding Australian outback. They had been in a romantic and artistic partnership since 1975, developing performance pieces that tested the physical and psychological limits of the human body. Their works involved such feats as sitting motionless for hours or breathing into each other's mouths until, due to lack of oxygen, they fell unconscious. According to Abramović, the 1980 trip to Australia inspired them to develop a massively ambitious performance piece called *The Lovers*, which focused on overcoming a new kind of endurance test. Both would walk along the Great Wall of China from opposite directions (a distance of some 2,500 km or 1,550 miles each) and meet in the middle, where, as originally planned, they would get married.

The Lovers, however, took far longer to accomplish than they expected. Bureaucratic hold-ups from the Chinese government, along with rigorous planning on their part, delayed the walk for eight years. By the time their Chinese journey began, in 1988, their personal relationship had ended, and marriage was out of the question. Nonetheless, both artists were determined to carry through with their plans. Abramović trekked over hundreds of miles of rocky, mountainous terrain – often having to walk several miles away from the Great Wall to find shelter in villages at night. Ulay trudged across parts of the wall in the Gobi Desert, experiencing similar levels of physical stress and hardship. When they finally met in the 'middle' in Shenmu, Shaanxi province, the exhausted pair embraced. But the emotion of the moment would not reignite their old love. Ulay later admitted that he had had a relationship with his female Chinese interpreter on the journey, one that resulted in a child. He and Abramović would not see each other again in person for more than twenty years – when Ulay unexpectedly attended Abramović's mammoth 2010 retrospective at New York's Museum of Modern Art (MoMA): *The Artist Is Present*.

The image shown here is an art piece Abramović made in 1996 to commemorate her Great Wall walk. The dramatic photographic print, which captures the daunting nature of her journey, is joined to a drawing of two pairs of empty shoes. It is a fitting tribute to the love one has for one's art, even when romantic love has faded.

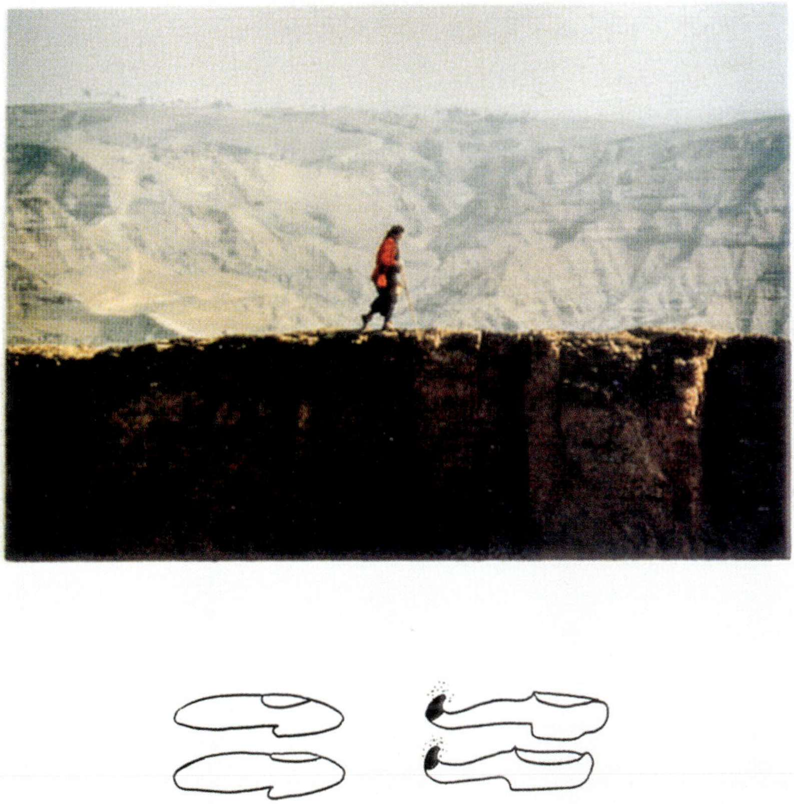

The Lovers, 1988/1996, twelve chromogenic prints with ink drawings in lower margin, 73 × 68.6 cm (28 ¾ × 27 in.)

JEFF KOONS
born 1955

Ilona and I were born for each other.
She's a media woman.
I'm a media man.
We are the contemporary Adam and Eve.

JEFF KOONS ON HIS *MADE IN HEAVEN* SERIES (1992)

In his controversial *Made in Heaven* series (1989–1992), Jeff Koons revels in the commodified 1980s world of love and sex. Koons was one of many American artists who made their way to New York in the wake of the Pop Art movement. Like Pop Art masters Andy Warhol (1928–1987) and Roy Lichtenstein (1923–1997), Koons was fascinated by popular culture, especially the elements of that culture considered banal or kitschy. He soon became famous for large-scale art exhibits that focused on a single image or idea, and that included numerous pieces in different media. These individual works were created by an array of associates and craftsmen who worked in Koons's studio, but it was Koons himself who devised the concept – and who took the credit – for the overall exhibits.

Made in Heaven was inspired by Koons's interest in the porn film industry. In 1989, when the Whitney Museum of American Art in New York asked Koons to make a billboard for an upcoming exhibition, he decided to create a fake movie poster featuring himself and an Italian porn star named Ilona Staller (who went by the stage name 'La Cicciolina'). The fake movie was given the title 'Made in Heaven', and the billboard showed Koons and Staller lying together on a rocky ground. Koons appears in the nude looking up at the camera, while Staller, dressed mostly in a frilly bra and stockings, assumes a look of fake ecstasy.

This campy send-up of pornography inspired Koons to develop the 'Made in Heaven' theme into a full-blown exhibition, which would feature marble and polychrome sculpture, photographs and other objects. Most of these works, meticulously rendered by craftsmen in Europe, would depict kitschy images of Koons and Staller, as well as cherub heads, flowers and other 'symbols' of love. The work shown here is a sculptural version, in garish polychromed wood, of the original '*Made in Heaven*' billboard. It is a fully commercialized image of love, an 'Adam and Eve' – complete with serpent – for the mass media age. The *Made in Heaven* exhibition divided critics, but it did lead to a real-life pledge of love between Koons and Staller, who were married in 1991. The marriage ended some three years later.

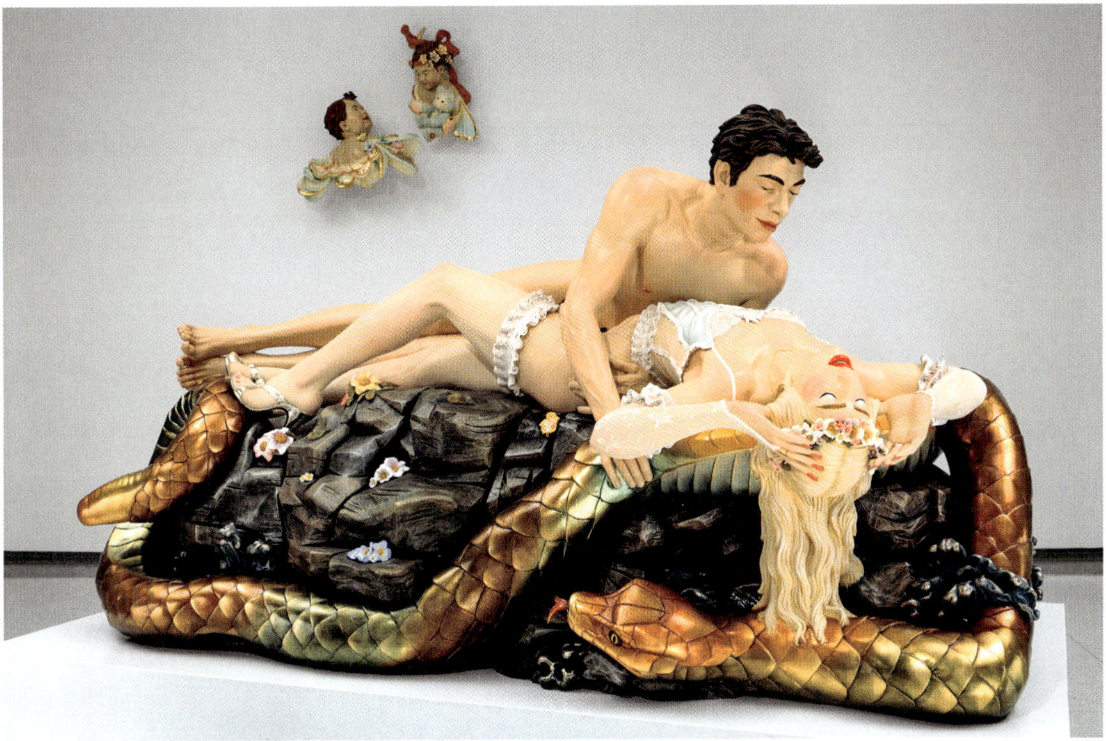

Jeff and Ilona (Made in Heaven), 1990, polychromed wood,
167.6 × 289.6 × 162.6 cm (66 × 114 × 64 in.), Private Collection

BANKSY

date of birth unknown

*I like to think I have the guts to stand up anonymously
in a western democracy
and call for things no-one else believes in –
like peace and justice and freedom.*

BANKSY, *WALL AND PIECE* (2005)

Love and war are intertwined in this iconic mural by British artist Banksy. The world's most famous street artist, Banksy's true identity has been kept secret for more than three decades. Though he initially chose such anonymity to avoid arrest (graffiti remains illegal in many countries), over time his fame and art have become closely linked with his mysterious persona. The discovery of a new Banksy mural is now a major story in the art world, especially as much of his work is infused with contemporary political messages.

Banksy has visited Israel and the Palestinian territories on several occasions. On his 2003 trip to Jerusalem and nearby villages, he painted this dramatic mural to promote peace in a troubled region. The early 2000s saw Israel's construction of the West Bank barrier, a 708-kilometre (440-mile) wall separating Israel from the Palestinian West Bank. Near this wall lies Beit Sahour, a town long populated by both Christian and Muslim Arabs, and which has been occupied by Israeli forces since 1967. Beit Sahour has become a centre of activism for Palestinian independence, with some of its local groups promoting non-violent resistance to Israeli occupation.

It was in this climate that Banksy secretly spray-painted *Love Is in the Air* on the wall of a local garage in Beit Sahour. The masked man, with his cap on backwards, resembles anti-war protesters of Banksy's generation. But instead of a rock or Molotov cocktail, the protester has a bouquet of flowers in his throwing hand – possibly a reference to photos from the 1960s that showed 'flower children' handing bouquets to troops bound for the Vietnam War. Though one can interpret *Love Is in the Air* as a cynical condemnation of endless Middle Eastern conflict, the work also suggests the potential 'power of love' and non-violence to overcome political division. These hopeful qualities have helped make it a widely reproduced image, and Banksy has sold numerous screenprint versions of the piece. Sadly, however, peace between Israelis and Palestinians remains elusive.

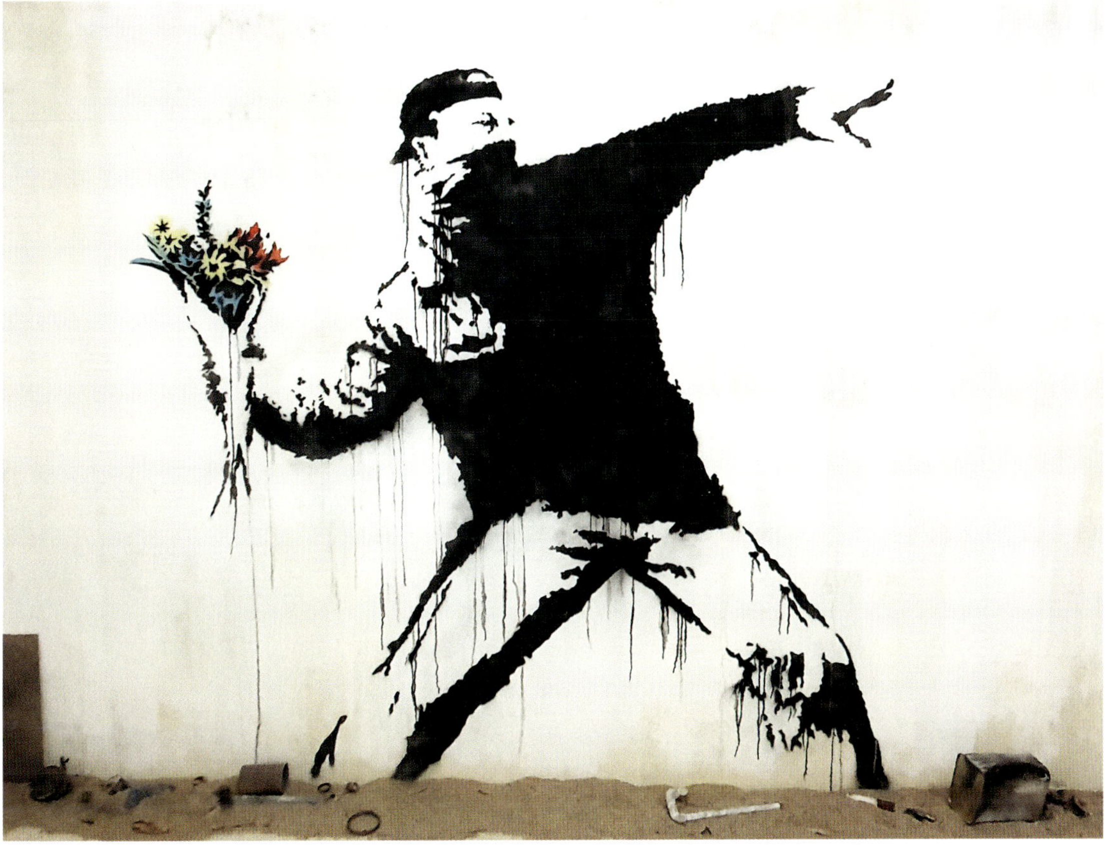

Love Is in the Air (Flower Thrower), 2003,
spray-painted mural on a garage wall, Beit Sahour

NJIDEKA AKUNYILI CROSBY
born 1983

Little love, little love,
On my journey of love, only a little remains.

NELLY UCHENDU,
LYRICS FROM 'LOVE NWANTINTI' (1976)

In her work *Nwantinti*, Nigerian-born artist Njideka Akunyili Crosby links romantic intimacy with references to the larger world of pop culture. The image's title derives from a popular 1970s love song in Igbo by Nigerian singer-songwriter Nelly Uchendu (1950–2005), a song Akunyili Crosby referred to as 'slang for cheesy, sappy love'.

Though at first glance *Nwantinti* seems to be a straightforward painting, closer inspection shows elements of different media. Most prominently, we see Akunyili Crosby's signature use of photo transfer collage. Bits of old black-and-white and colour Xerox photocopies have been carefully cut to form the outlines and shapes of the walls, bedspread and carpet, as well as the reclining male figure. By contrast, Akunyili Crosby uses a more traditional painting technique to render the woman, who sits over the man with his head in her lap. In this way, the female character is given a rounder, more substantial appearance – she is the one in control. Yet there is no hint of sexual dominance here. Akunyili Crosby allows the viewer to witness a tender, meditative moment in the lives of this couple. She even shows us the woman's clothing hanging in her closet, heightening the scene's intimate nature. In interviews, Akunyili Crosby refers to *Nwantinti* as reflecting her life with her Texas-born husband, though the couple in the picture are not necessarily meant to be portraits.

Amidst this intimacy, we are also meant to look carefully at the details of Akunyili Crosby's collage. Individual Xerox images include pictures of the original 'Nwantinti' album cover from 1976, as well as family photos from Akunyili Crosby's childhood. Such details link the affectionate man and woman with the artist's Nigerian roots. Romantic love is closely bound up with love of one's heritage.

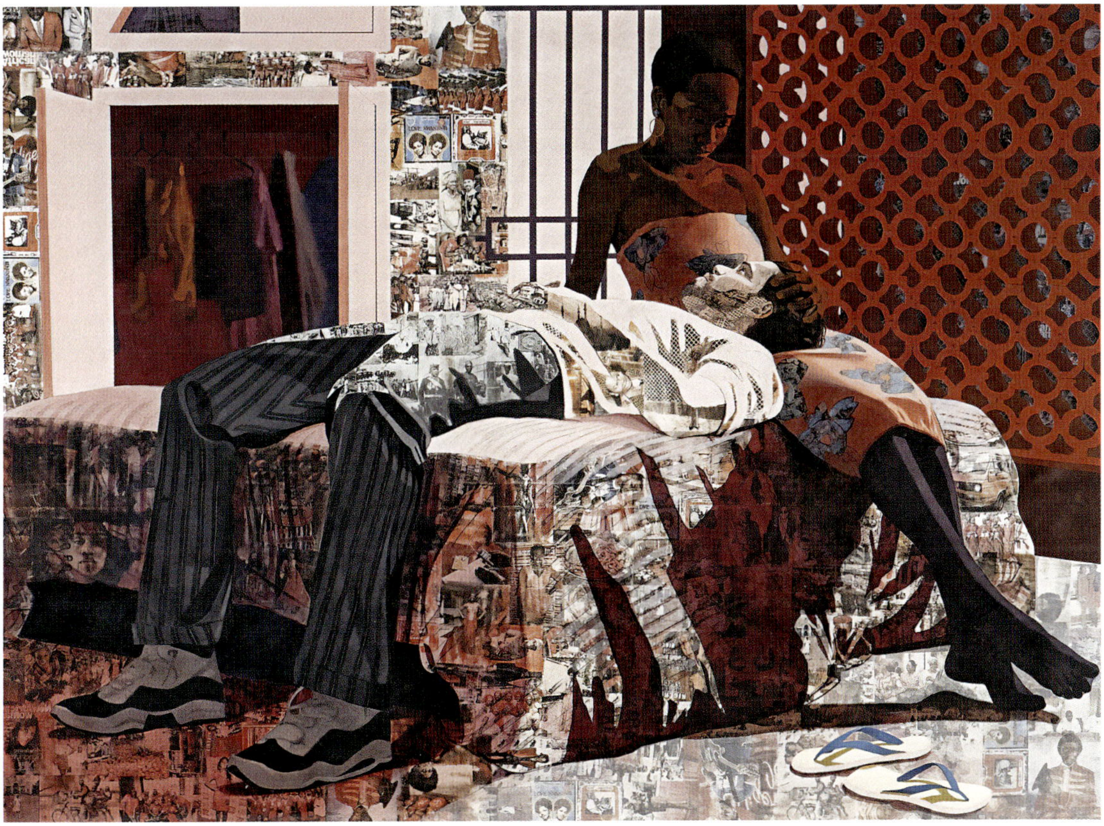

Nwantinti, 2012, acrylic, pastel, charcoal, coloured pencil and Xerox transfers on paper, 172.7 × 243.8 cm (68 × 96 in.), Studio Museum in Harlem, New York

YAYOI KUSAMA

born 1929

[...] I have lived through to this day
Hoping to leave beautiful footprints at the end of my life
I spend each day praying that my wish will be fulfilled
This is my message of love to you

YAYOI KUSAMA, FROM HER POEM
'RESIDING IN A CASTLE OF SHED TEARS' (2010)

Themes of love and mortality become an immersive experience in Japanese artist Yayoi Kusama's installation, *Love is Calling*, first exhibited in 2013. Kusama's epic life (now more than nine decades old) began during the war. As a teenager, she sewed parachutes for the Japanese army in World War II. She also experienced unhappiness in her family life, a hardship made worse by bouts of mental illness, which included hallucinations and thoughts of suicide.

After struggling as an artist for several years in postwar Japan, she moved to the United States, eventually settling in New York in 1958. There she befriended many of the city's most prominent artists, including Joseph Cornell (1903–1972, with whom she had a long-term affair), Claes Oldenburg (1929–2022) and Andy Warhol (1928–1987). Kusama dabbled in almost every artistic field, from poetry to performance art to fashion, but she became best known for her large art installations. These room-sized exhibits are decorated with mirrors, lights or twisting sculptures made with soft material and covered in polka dots, the artist's signature image. Sometimes they also include sounds – music or poetry – piped in through speakers, creating an experience that engages all the viewer's senses. Kusama's kaleidoscopic rooms may reflect, in part, her own experiences with hallucinations.

The work shown here, *Love is Calling*, captures all of the elements in Kusama's installation art. It was created after she moved back to Japan, where she still lives today. For Kusama, the work represents a 'castle of shed tears', as she describes it in the poem that visitors hear as they walk through the exhibit. It is an embodiment of her decades-long search for love – and her coming to terms with her own mortality.

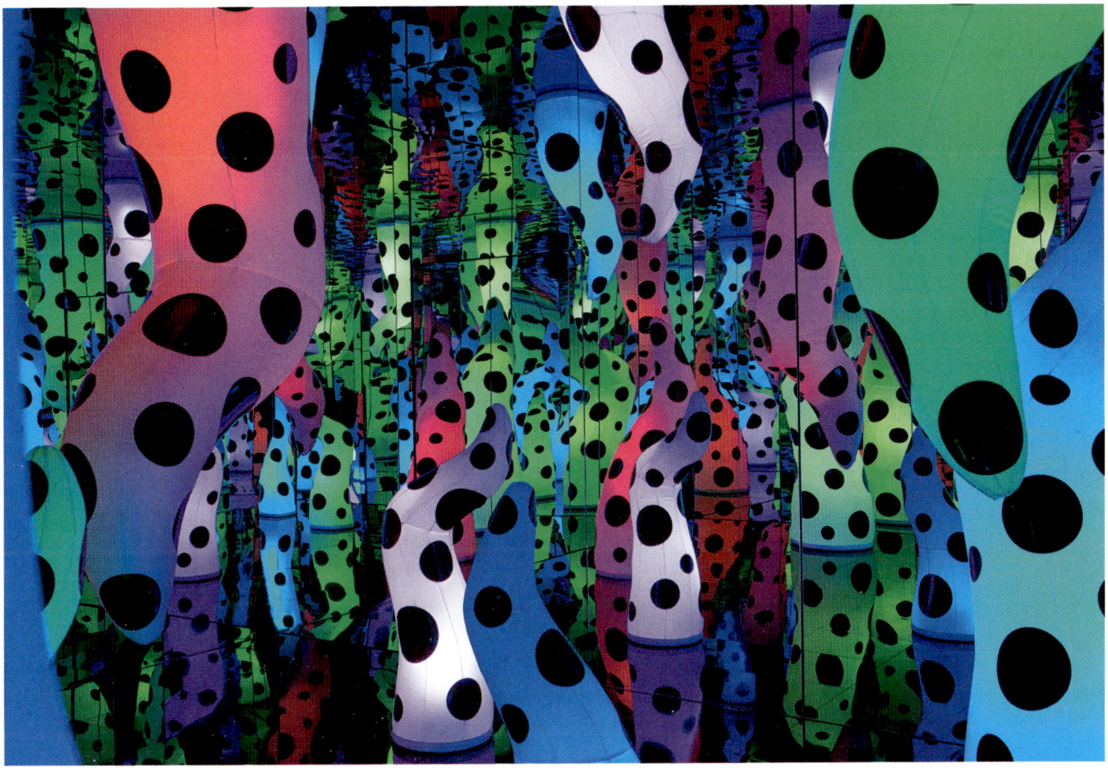

Love is Calling, 2013, wood, metal, glass mirrors, tiles, acrylic panels, rubber, blowers, lighting elements, speakers and sound, 443.2 × 865.2 × 608 cm (174 ½ × 340 ⅝ × 239 ⅜ in.), Institute of Contemporary Art, Boston

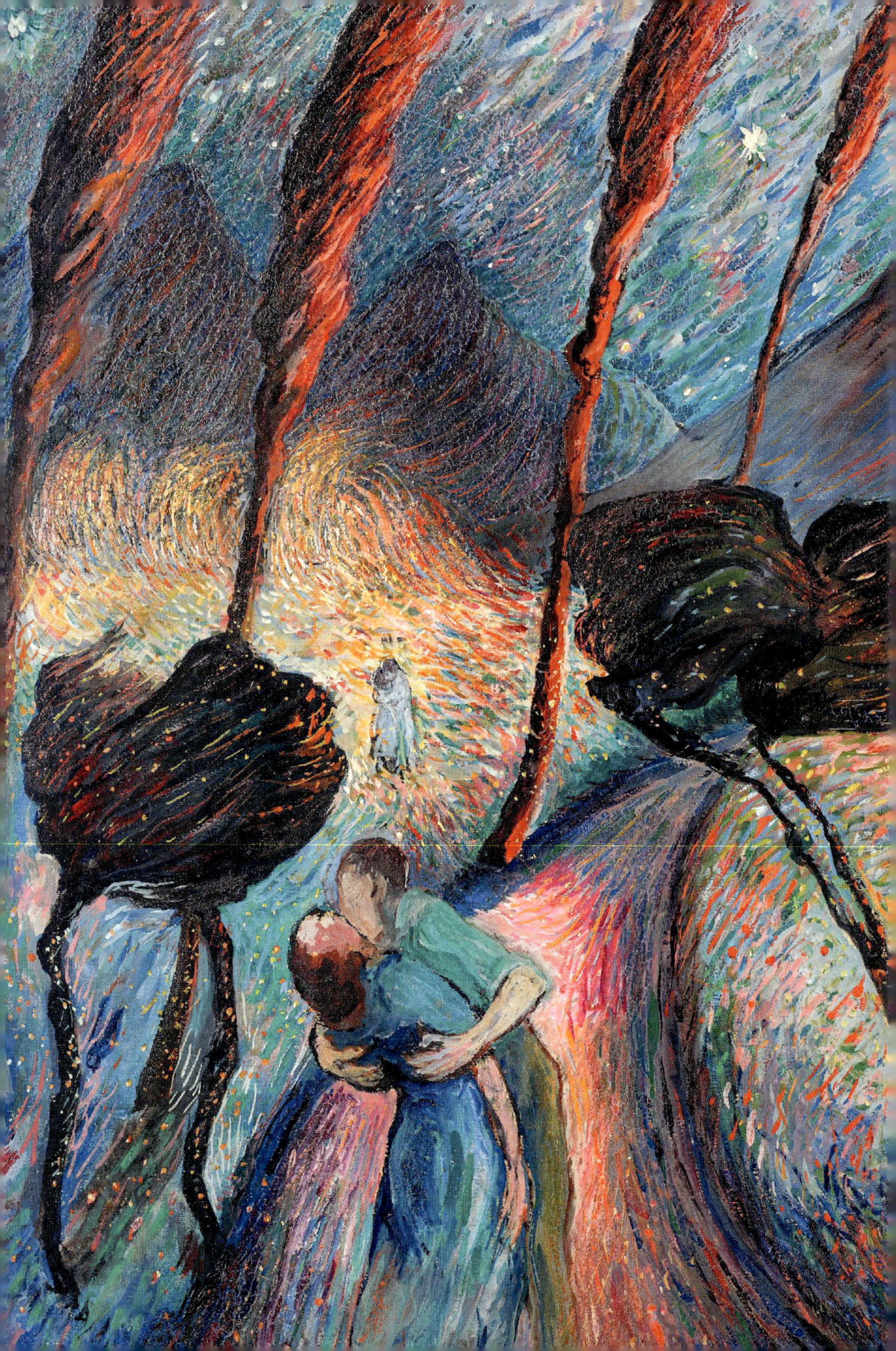

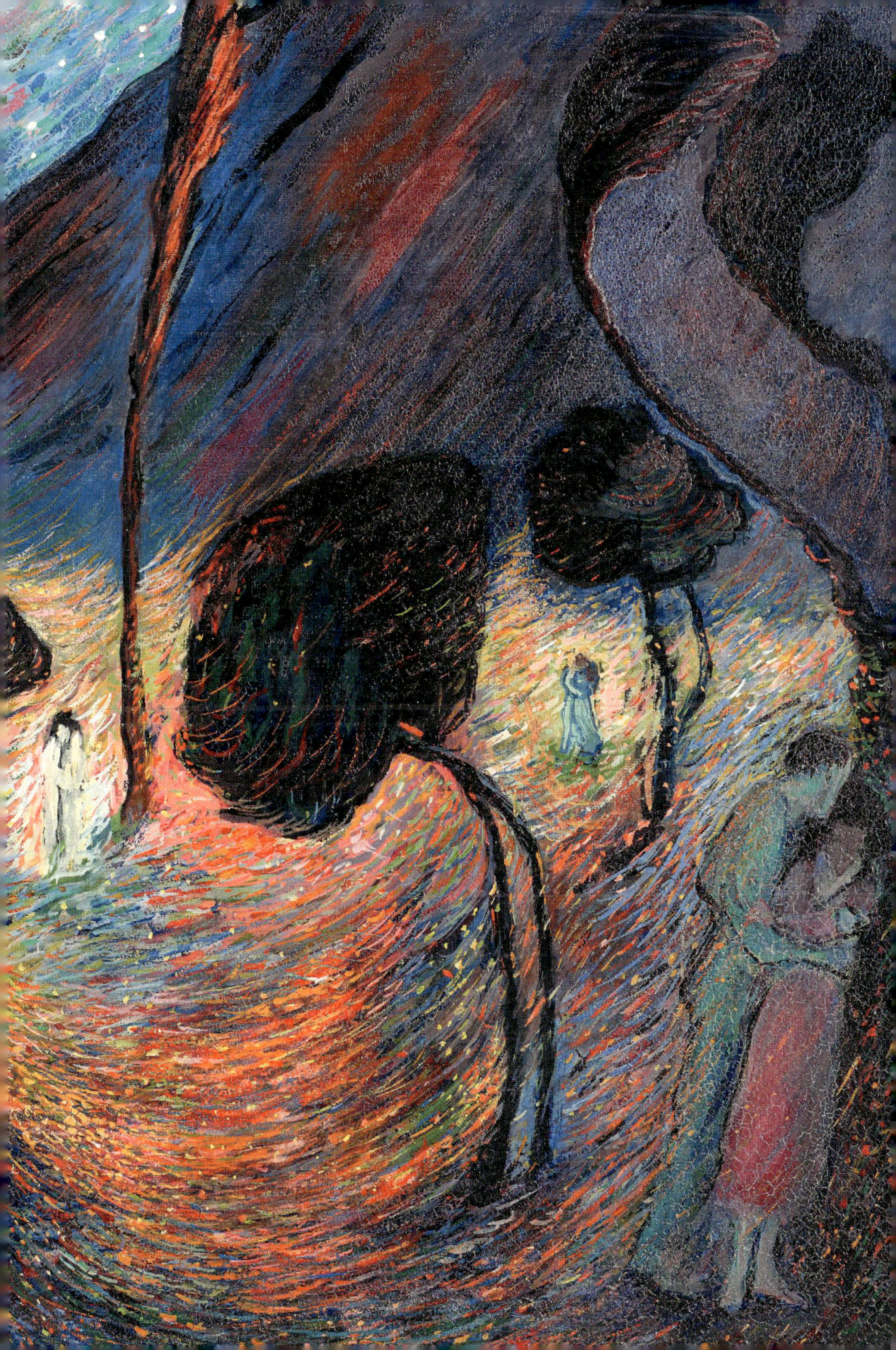

SOURCES OF QUOTATIONS

p. 9 Johann Wolfgang von Goethe, *The Sorrows of Young Werther*, trans. R. D. Boylan, ed. Nathan Haskell Dole (1854; Boston: Francis A. Niccolls & Co., c. 1902), p. 23.

p. 14 Akhenaten, speech from the early part of his reign (c. 1350 BC), recorded on a pylon at the Karnak temple complex, documented in Donald B. Redford, 'A Royal Speech from the Blocks of the Tenth Pylon', *Bulletin of the Egyptological Seminar* 3 (1981): pp. 87–102, qtd. in Dominic Perry, *History of Egypt*, podcast, episode 110, 'The Aten Appears', 15 May 2019, https://www.egyptianhistorypodcast.com/the-aten-appears-episode-110/.

p. 16 Pseudo-Lucian, *Affairs of the Heart (Amores)*, in *Lucian*, vol. 8, trans. M. D. Macleod, Loeb Classical Library 432 (Cambridge, MA: Harvard University Press; London: William Heinemann, 1967), pp. 169, 171.

p. 18 Giovanni Boccaccio, *Genealogie deorum gentilium*, book 5, chapter 22, stanza 10; see *Genealogy of the Pagan Gods*, vol. 1, books 1–5, ed. Jon Solomon, I Tatti Renaissance Library 46 (Cambridge, MA: Harvard University Press, 2011), pp. 694–695, 787.

p. 20 Konrad von Altstetten, 'Ich hân mîn herze der lieben gesendet', in *Bibliothek Älterer Schriftwerke der deutschen Schweiz*, vol. 6, *Die Schweizer Minnesänger*, ed. Jakob Baechtold and Ferdinand Vetter (Frauenfeld: J. Huber, 1887), pp. 265–266.

p. 22 Petrarch, Sonnet 13, in *The Complete Canzoniere*, trans. A. S. Kline (2002), Poetry in Translation, https://www.poetryintranslation.com/PITBR/Italian/PetrarchCanzoniere001-061.php.

p. 24 *Homeric Hymn to Aphrodite*, trans. Gregory Nagy, Center for Hellenic Studies, Harvard University, https://chs.harvard.edu/primary-source/homeric-hymn-to-aphrodite-sb/.

p. 26 Genesis 6:5 (New International Version, NIV).

p. 30 Isaiah 40:7 (NIV).

p. 32 Marsilio Ficino, *Commentary on Plato's Symposium (De amore)*, qtd. in John Vyvyan, *Shakespeare and Platonic Beauty* (1961; New York: Barnes and Noble, 1970), p. 48.

p. 34 Genesis 3:6 (NIV).

p. 36 Ovid, *Metamorphoses*, book I, lines 587–600, trans. A. S. Kline (2000), University of Virginia Library, https://ovid.lib.virginia.edu/trans/Metamorph.htm.

p. 38 Giorgio Vasari, *Lives of the Most Excellent Painters, Sculptors, and Architects*, vol. 2, *Part III – Continued*, trans. Gaston du C. de Vere (1912; New York: Everyman's Library, 1996), p. 872.

p. 40 Lodovico Guicciardini, *The Description of the Low countreys and of the Prouinces thereof* [...] (London, 1593), p. 15, https://quod.lib.umich.edu/e/eebo2/A02335.0001.001.

p. 42 Ovid, *Metamorphoses*, book III, lines 402–436 and 474–510, trans. A. S. Kline (2000), University of Virginia Library, https://ovid.lib.virginia.edu/trans/Metamorph3.htm.

p. 44 Peter Paul Rubens, letter to Pierre Dupuy, 15 July 1626, in *The Letters of Peter Paul Rubens*, ed. and trans. Ruth Saunders Magurn (Cambridge, MA: Harvard University Press, 1955), p. 136.

p. 46 Judges 16:15–17 and 19 (NIV).

p. 48 Stephan Koja, qtd. in Tessa Solomon, 'Restoration of Vermeer Painting in Germany Reveals Hidden Image of Cupid', *ARTnews*, 24 August 2021, https://www.artnews.com/art-news/news/vermeer-girl-reading-a-letter-cupid-restoration-1234602227/.

p. 50 Edmond and Jules de Goncourt, *L'Art du XVIIIe siècle*, qtd. in Ettore Camesasca, *The Complete Paintings of Watteau* (New York: Harry N. Abrams, 1968), p. 12.

p. 52 *Brahma-Vaivarta Purana*, trans. Rajendra Nath Sen, vol. XXIV of *The Sacred Books of the Hindus*, ed. B. D. Basu (Bahadurganj: Sudhindra Nath Vasu, 1922), p. 547.

p. 55 Charles Collé, journal entry, October 1767, qtd. in 'Origins of *The Swing*: The Commission', The Wallace Collection, https://www.wallacecollection.org/explore/explore-in-depth/fragonards-the-swing/origins-of-the-swing/the-commission/.

p. 58 James Thomson, 'Spring', from *The Seasons* (1730), in *The Complete Poetical Works of James Thomson*, ed. J. Logie Robertson (London: Henry Frowde of Oxford University Press, 1908), lines 936–940, p. 38. Also, Joshua Reynolds, 'Discourse XIV', 10 December 1788, in *Sir Joshua Reynolds's Discourses*, ed. Edward Gilpin Johnson (Chicago: A. C. McClurg, 1891), p. 343.

p. 60 Mary Cassatt, letter to Bertha Morisot, 1890, qtd. in *Mary Cassatt: The Color Prints*, ed. Nancy Mowll Mathews and Barbara Stern Shapiro (New York: Harry N. Abrams, 1989), p. 36.

p. 62 Jane Austen, *Persuasion* (1817), ed. Gillian Beer (1998; London: Penguin, 2003), p. 66.

p. 64 Defendente Sacchi, 'Del bello e del Brutto', from Article VI, 'Un provinciale a Milano – Visita allo studio di Hayez', in *Miscellanea di lettre ed arti* (Pavia: Bizzoni, 1830), p. 175, qtd. in Laura L. Watts, *Italian Painting in the Age of Unification* (New York: Routledge, 2021), p. 116.

p. 66 Joris-Karl Huysmans, 'Le Salon officiel de 1880', pt. 4, *La Réforme*, vol. 2 (1 July 1880), reprinted in Huysmans, *L'Art moderne* (Paris: Librairie Plon, 1883), pp. 174–175, qtd. in Michel Hoog, 'The Père Lathuile Restaurant', trans. Richard A. H. Oxby, in *Impressionism: A Century Exhibition*, exh. cat. (New York: Metropolitan Museum, 1974), p. 129. Also, Pierre Courthion, *Édouard Manet* (New York: Harry N. Abrams, 1984), p. 114.

p. 68 Pierre-Auguste Renoir, in conversation with Ambroise Vollard, *Renoir: An Intimate Record*, trans. Harold L. van Doren and Randolph T. Weaver (New York: Alfred A. Knopf, 1925), p. 49.

p. 70 Auguste Rodin's 'Testament' dictated to Paul Gsell (1911), published in *Histoire Générale de l'art français de la Révolution à nos jours*, vol. 2, *L'Architecture et La Sculpture*, by André Fontainas and Louis Vauxcelles (Paris, Librairie de France, 1922), p. 261, qtd. in Herbert Read, *A Concise History of Modern Sculpture* (New York: Frederick A. Praeger, 1964), p. 14.

p. 72 Catullus 45, from 'Acme and Septimius', in *The Poems of Catullus*, trans. Theodore Martin (London: Parker Son and Bourn, 1861), p. 52, used in *The Exhibition of the Royal Academy of Arts* (London: William Clowes and Sons, 1868), p. 25.

p. 75 Thadée Natanson, 'Petite Gazette d'art: De M. Félix Vallotton', *La Revue blanche*, 1 January 1899, qtd. in Sasha M. Newman, '"Stages of Sentimental Life": The Nudes and the Interiors', in *Félix Vallotton*, exh. cat. (New Haven, CT: Yale University Art Gallery; New York: Abbeville, 1991), p. 141.

p. 78 Edvard Munch, sketchbook, MM T 2759, fol. 7r, undated, eMunch: Edvard Munch's Writing, https://emunch.no/TRANS_HYBRIDMM_T2759.xhtml, qtd. in Iris Müller-Westermann, 'The Dance of Life', in *Edvard Munch: The Frieze of Life*, exh. cat., ed. Mara-Helen Wood (London: National Gallery, 1992), p. 78.

p. 80 Jeanne Robert Foster (née Julia Elizabeth Oliver), 'New Sculptures by Constantin Brancusi', *Vanity Fair*, May 1922, p. 68. Also, Sidney Geist, *Brancusi: A Study of the Sculpture* (New York: Grossman, 1967), p. 141.

p. 82 Louis Vauxcelles, 'Le Salon des indépendants', *Gil Blas*, 20 March 1906, reprinted in *Matisse: A Retrospective*, ed. Jack Flam (New York: Hugh Lauter Levin, 1988), p. 52.

p. 84 Wilhelm Dessauer, 'Gustav Klimts Winterreise nach Italien: Unveröffentlichte Erinnerungen des Malers Lenz, mitgeteilt von Wilhelm Dessauer', *Österreichische Kunst* 4, no. 3 (1933), pp. 11–12, qtd. in Frank Whitford, *Gustav Klimt* (London: Collins & Brown, 1993), p. 86.

p. 86 Gabriele Münter, interviewed by Edouard Roditi (1958), in *Conversations with European Artists at Mid-Century* (London: Lund Humphries, 1990), p. 120.

p. 88 Marc Chagall, *My Life* (1923), trans. Elisabeth Abbott (New York: Orion, 1960), p. 74.

p. 90 Marianne von Werefkin, notebook 1, fol. 29, in *Lettres à un inconnu: Aux sources de l'expressionnisme*, ed. Gabrielle Dufour-Kowalska (Paris: Klincksieck, 1999), p. 75.

p. 92 Geneviève Laporte, *Sunshine at Midnight: Memories of Picasso and Cocteau* (1973), trans. Douglas Cooper (London: Weidenfeld and Nicolson, 1975), p. 12.

p. 94 Paul Klee, 'The Concept of Artistic Creation', in *Paul Klee Notebooks*, vol. 1, *The Thinking Eye* (1956), ed. Jürg Spiller, trans. Ralph Manheim (1961; London: Lund Humphries, 1973), p. 17.

p. 97 Frequently attributed to René Magritte; see DaeQuan Alexander Collier 'Surreal Love: Unveiling René Magritte's *The Lovers*; Love is blind...and suffocating?', *MoMA: Magazine*, 7 February 2024, https://www.moma.org/magazine/articles/1018.

p. 100 Grant Wood, questioned in Dorothy Dougherty, 'The Right and Wrong of America', *Cedar Rapids Gazette*, 6 September 1942, qtd. in Steven Biel, *American Gothic: A Life of America's Most Famous Painting*, pp. 60–61.

p. 102 Man Ray, 'à l'heure de l'observatoire ... les amoureux', *Cahiers d'art* 10, nos. 5–6 (1935): p. 127, translated as 'at observatory time ... the lovers', in Man Ray, *Writings on Art*, ed. Jennifer Mundy (Los Angeles: Getty Research Institute, 2016), pp. 128–129.

p. 104 Frida Kahlo, letter to Sigmund Firestone, 1 November 1940, qtd. in Hayden Herrera, *Frida: A Biography of Frida Kahlo* (New York: Harper & Row, 1983), p. 299.

p. 106 Gerhard Richter, interviewed by Wolfgang Pehnt, in *German Art Now* (London: Academy Edition; New York: St. Martin, 1989), p. 50.

p. 108 Robert Indiana, interviewed by Jeff Goldberg, 'Love', *Unmuzzled Ox* 4, no. 2 (1976): p. 19, qtd. in Susan Elizabeth Ryan, *Robert Indiana: Figures of Speech* (New Haven, CT: Yale University Press, 200), p. 235. Also, Indiana, interviewed by Ryan (1990), for *Robert Indiana: Figures of Speech*, p. 206.

p. 110 Keith Haring, interviewed by John Gruen (1990), *Keith Haring: The Authorized Biography* (New York: Fireside, 1991), p. 187.

p. 112 Marina Abramović, artist statement, *The Lovers (4 Shoes)*, 1988/1996, Schwartz Art Collection, Harvard Business School, https://www.hbs.edu/about/campus-and-culture/contemporary-art/schwartz-art-collection/list/abramovicmarina1.

p. 114 Jeff Koons in *The Jeff Koons Handbook*, introduction by Robert Rosenblum (New York: Rizzoli, 1992), p. 140.

p. 116 Banksy, *Banksy: Wall and Piece* (London: Century, 2005), p. 24.

p. 118 Nelly Uchendu, 'Love Nwantinti', feat. Mike Obianwu, Homzy Records (1976); for an interlinear translation see Adaeze Wosu, The Igbo Music Project, 29 November 2010, https://igbomusicproject.wordpress.com/2010/11/29/love-nwantinti-by-nelly-uchendu/. Also, Akunyili Crosby interviewed by Cheryl Brutvan, in *Njideka Akunyili Crosby: I Refuse to be Invisible*, exh. cat., ed. Brutvan (West Palm Beach: Norton Museum of Art, 2016).

p. 120 Yayoi Kusama, 'Residing in a Castle of Shed Tears', poem used in the installation *Love is Calling*, qtd. in Julie Tremaine, 'Inside New England's First-Ever Permanent Yayoi Kusama Infinity Room', *Forbes*, 30 November 2019, https://www.forbes.com/sites/julietremaine/2019/11/30/inside-new-englands-first-ever-permanent-yayoi-kusama-infinity-room/.

For this publication, the translations of Konrad von Altstetten, Boccaccio and Werefkin are by José Enrique Macián y Fijałkowski.

IMAGE CREDITS

p. 15: Staatliche Museen zu Berlin, Ägyptisches Museum und Papyrussammlung / Margarete Büsing CC BY-SA 4.0; p. 17: Metropolitan Museum of Art, New York, CC0; p. 19: Mondadori Portfolio/Archivio Dell'arte Luciano Pedicini/Luciano Pedicini / Bridgeman Images; p. 21: CC0; p. 23: CC0; p. 25: CC0; pp. 26/27: CC0; p. 31: CC0; pp. 32/33: CC0; p. 35: CC0; p. 37: CC0; p. 39: CC0; p. 41: CC0; p. 43: CC0; p. 45: Bayerische Staatsgemäldesammlungen – Alte Pinakothek München, URL: https://www.sammlung.pinakothek.de/de/artwork/o5xrMEr47X; p. 47: CC0; p. 49: © Gemäldegalerie Alte Meister, Staatliche Kunstsammlungen Dresden / Bridgeman Images; p. 51: CC0; p. 53: CC0; p. 54: CC0; p. 59: CC0; p. 61: CC0; p. 63: CC0; p. 65: CC0; p. 67: Édouard Manet artist QS:P170,Q40599 Sailko (https://commons.wikimedia.org/wiki/File:Edouard_manet,_chez_le_père_lathuille,_1879,_01.jpg), 'Edouard manet, chez le père lathuille, 1879, 01', https://creativecommons.org/licenses/by/3.0/legalcode; p. 69: CC0; p. 71: Fine Art Images/ARTOTHEK; p. 73: CC0; p. 74: © Photo Josse / Bridgeman Images; p. 79: Nasjonalmuseet/Børre Høstland, CC0; p. 81: Copyright © Christie's Images Ltd / Photo © Christie's Images Ltd, ARTOTHEK; p. 83: The Barnes Foundation, BF719, CC0; p. 85: CC0; p. 87: bpk / Städtische Galerie im Lenbachhaus und Kunstbau München; p. 89: Superstock / Bridgeman Images; p. 91: CC0; p. 93: © Succession Picasso/DACS, London 2026 / Bridgeman Images; p. 95: akg-images; p. 96: Luisa Ricciarini / Bridgeman Images; p. 101: CC0; p. 103: © Albright-Knox Art Gallery, akg-images; p. 105: © Fine Art Images / Bridgeman Images; p. 107: © Gerhard Richter 2026 (0084); p. 109: Digital image, The Museum of Modern Art, New York/Scala, Florence; p. 111: arthipo; p. 113: © Marina Abramović Courtesy of the Marina Abramović Archives; p. 115: Jeff Koons LLC; p. 117: CC0; p. 119: The Studio Museum in Harlem; Museum purchase with funds provided by the Acquisition Committee and gift of the artist; p. 121: Institute of Contemporary Art, Boston.

A member of Penguin Random House Verlagsgruppe GmbH
Neumarkter Strasse 28 · 81673 Munich

1st edition 2026

produktsicherheit@penguinrandomhouse.de

Front Cover: Gustav Klimt, *The Kiss*, 1908/09: p. 85

Details: pp. 6/7: p. 51; pp. 12/13: p. 89; pp. 28/29: pp. 26/27; pp. 56/57: p. 54; pp. 76/77: p. 74; pp. 98/99: p. 96; pp. 122/123: p. 91.

A CIP catalogue record for this book is available from the British Library.
Library of Congress Control Number is available.

Editorial Direction Prestel: Markus Eisen
Copy-Editing: José Enrique Macián y Fijałkowski

Design and Layout: April, Joana Niemeyer
Production Management: Martina Effaga
Separations: Reproline Mediateam GmbH, Unterföhring
Printing: TBB, Banská Bystrica
Typeface: Certeau Pro, Canela, Figue
Paper: 170 g/m², Magno Volume

Printed in the Slovak Republic

ISBN 978-3-7913-9467-1 (English Edition)
ISBN 978-3-7913-9466-4 (German Edition)

www.prestel.com